ROUTE 66 TRAVEL GUIDE 2025

The Ultimate Road Trip Planner with Maps, Must-See Attractions, Historic Landmarks, Scenic Drives, and Hidden Gems from Chicago to Santa Monica

Richard K. Brice

Copyright © 2025 (Richard K. Brice)

All rights reserved. No part of this book may be reproduced or transmitted in any form or by any means, electronic or mechanical, including photocopying, recording or by any information storage and retrieval system, without written permission from the author, except for the inclusion of brief quotations embodied in critical reviews and certain other non commercial uses permitted by copyright law.

DISCLAIMER

Welcome to the *Route 66 Travel Guide 2025*. While every effort has been made to provide accurate and up-to-date information, please note that details such as road conditions, seasonal hours, local regulations, and available services may change. We strongly recommend verifying current information with local authorities, service providers, or attractions before finalizing your travel plans. Stay informed, stay safe, and enjoy your unforgettable adventure along Route 66!

Table Of Contents

Introduction 7
Chapter 1: Welcome to Route 66 9
   Brief History 9
   How to Use This Guide 10
Chapter 2: Planning Your Route 66 Adventure 13
   Best Time to Travel 13
   Packing Essentials 15
Chapter 3: The Complete Route 66 Overview 17
   Key Route 66 States and Cities 17
Chapter 4: Iconic Stops Along Route 66 21
   Chicago, Illinois 21
   St. Louis, Missouri 26
   Tulsa, Oklahoma 32
   Amarillo, Texas 37
   Albuquerque, New Mexico 43
   Flagstaff, Arizona 49
   Santa Monica, California 55
Chapter 6: Local Culture and Traditions 61
   Small-Town America 61
Chapter 7: Accommodations 65
   Best Motels 65
   Best Hotels 71
   Best Campsites 79
Chapter 8: Dining 89
   Classic American Diners and Must-Try Meals 89
   Vegetarian and Vegan Options 91
   Unique Dining Experiences Along the Route 94
Chapter 9: Route 66 Road Trip Activities 97

Hiking and Outdoor Adventures...97
Local Shopping and Souvenir Spots...................................99
Photography Tips for Route 66..100
Family-Friendly Activities.. 101
Chapter 10: Itinerary Options..103
10-Day Adventure.. 103
Extended 2-3 Week Road Trip.......................................107
Weekend Getaway.. 108
Chapter 11: Practical Travel Tips....................................... 111
Navigating the Route.. 111
Gas Stations and Rest Stops... 112
Dealing with Weather and Emergencies........................... 113
Money-Saving Tips...115
Conclusion.. 117

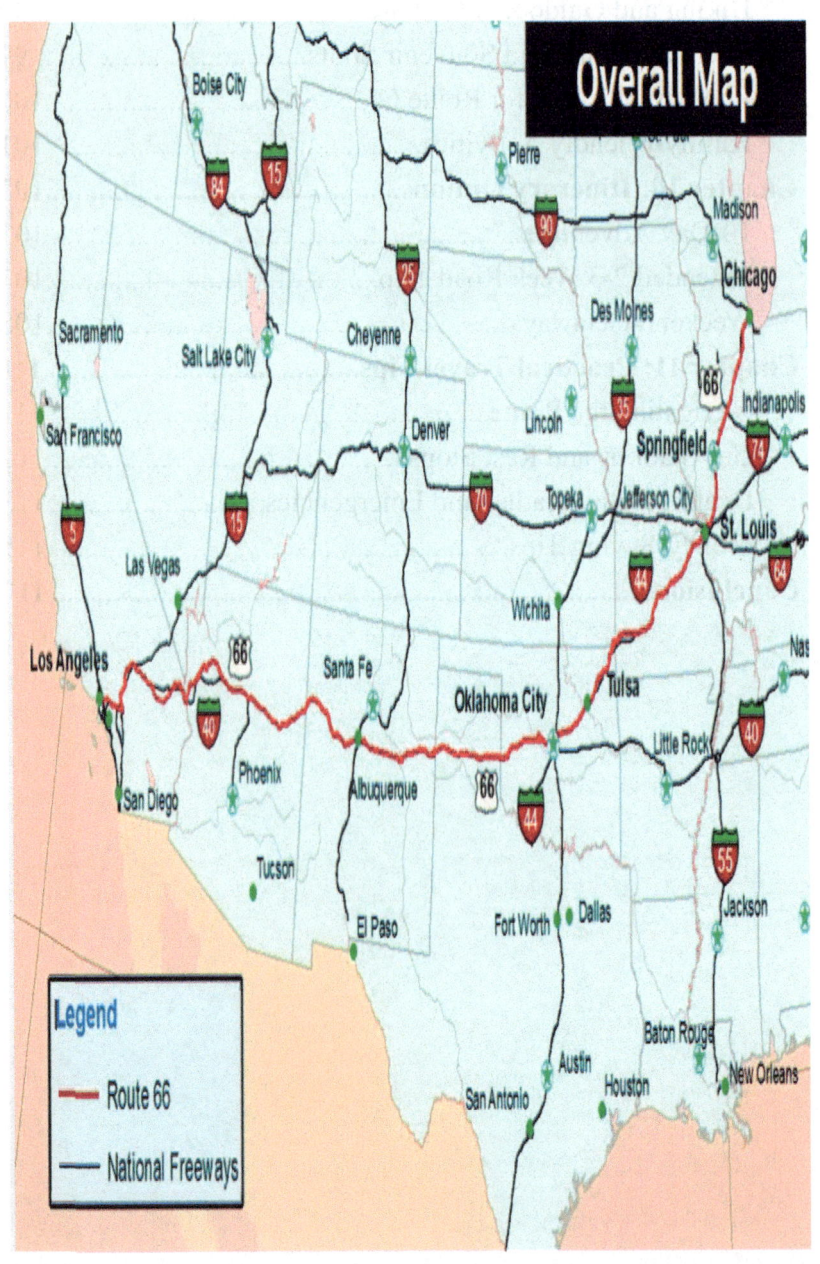

Introduction

As I set out on my own journey along Route 66, it felt like something truly magical was unfolding before me. Each mile brought new sights, sounds, and experiences that left me in awe of what this iconic highway represents. From the moment I left Chicago, I felt like I was stepping into a time capsule, with each small town offering its own unique story and charm. It's not just about the places; it's the people, the history, and the very essence of Americana that makes this route unforgettable.

I remember my first stop in St. Louis—standing under the Gateway Arch, I was filled with a sense of wonder, knowing I was about to experience one of the most famous roads in the world. The energy in each town was palpable. Amarillo, with its giant Cadillac Ranch, made me feel like I had stumbled into a road trip lover's dream. And don't even get me started on the quirky diners! I've never had a better burger in my life than at one of the local Route 66 gems in New Mexico.

The most surreal moments came when I was exploring some of the more hidden parts of the route. Like when I stumbled upon a forgotten stretch of highway lined with old gas stations and vintage signs that took me back to the glory days of Route 66. Or when I took a detour and found myself at a small museum that brought the history of this legendary route to life in a way that I hadn't expected.

But it wasn't just the iconic landmarks that made this trip so special—it was the feeling of being truly connected to the land. The vastness of the deserts, the rolling hills of Oklahoma, and the wide open skies in Arizona all gave me a sense of freedom that I hadn't realized I was craving.

By the time I reached Santa Monica, the end of the road, I felt like I had experienced something more than just a road trip. It was a journey of discovery—not just about the places I visited, but about myself. And I know that as you read this guide and start planning your own adventure, you'll feel that same sense of excitement, wonder, and connection.

So, let's dive in! This guide is a reflection of my own experiences, tips, and insights, meant to help you get the most out of your time on Route 66. Whether you're just starting your trip or planning the ultimate road trip, I hope my journey can inspire yours. The road is waiting!

Chapter 1: Welcome to Route 66

Welcome to Route 66, one of the most iconic highways in the world and a road trip experience like no other. Stretching from Chicago to Santa Monica, this legendary route is steeped in history, culture, and stories that have captivated travelers for decades.

Throughout the 20th century, Route 66 was the main artery of American road travel, drawing people from all walks of life to experience its charm. Today, even though much of the route has been replaced by modern interstate highways, the legacy of Route 66 remains alive through its well-preserved landmarks, vintage gas stations, quirky diners, and roadside attractions.

Brief History

Route 66, officially known as U.S. Highway 66, was one of the original highways in the United States Highway System, established in 1926. Spanning 2,448 miles, it connected eight states—Illinois, Missouri, Kansas, Oklahoma, Texas, New Mexico, Arizona, and California—and passed through a variety of landscapes, from the flat plains of the Midwest to the rugged deserts of the West.

The route became a lifeline for families and farmers migrating westward during the Dust Bowl and Great Depression, offering them a path to a new life in California. For many, Route 66 represented hope, opportunity, and a fresh start. The road gained widespread popularity as the automobile industry boomed, with travelers flocking to it for vacations, work, and escape.

In the 1950s and 1960s, Route 66 became synonymous with the American road trip. Classic cars, neon signs, motels, diners, and drive-in theaters dotted the landscape, creating an experience that became immortalized in movies, music, and pop culture. As the years went by and interstates replaced many stretches of the original highway, Route 66 was decommissioned in 1985, but its legend lived on. Today, Route 66 continues to draw those in search of adventure, nostalgia, and a connection to the past.

How to Use This Guide

This guide is your roadmap to an unforgettable adventure along the historic Route 66. It has been designed to provide you with all the essential information, tips, and insights you need to make the most of your journey. Whether you're traveling the entire length of the road or just exploring a few key stops, you'll find detailed descriptions of the must-see landmarks, hidden gems, and local attractions that define Route 66.

Each chapter of the guide is organized by state, starting with Illinois in the east and moving westward to California. Within each state section, you'll find recommendations for the best towns to visit, where to eat, where to stay, and the sights you can't miss. Alongside practical travel advice, we'll share the stories behind some of the most iconic locations and lesser-known treasures, bringing Route 66 to life in ways that will enhance your trip.

Throughout the guide, you'll also find helpful travel tips, including advice on navigating the route, seasonal considerations, and the best time to travel. The information is presented in a clear, easy-to-follow format so you can quickly access what you need, whether you're planning ahead or on the road.

So, grab your map, fuel up, and get ready to hit the road! Route 66 is waiting for you, and this guide will help you make the most of every mile.

Chapter 2: Planning Your Route 66 Adventure

Planning your Route 66 adventure is an exciting step. From choosing the best time to travel to understanding how to prepare for the road ahead, this chapter will equip you with all the tools you need to ensure your road trip is smooth, enjoyable, and full of memorable experiences.

Best Time to Travel

When planning your Route 66 adventure, selecting the optimal travel period is crucial to ensure a comfortable and enjoyable experience. The timing of your journey influences weather conditions, crowd sizes, and the availability of services along the route.

Spring (Late April to June): Late spring offers mild temperatures and vibrant scenery. Traveling during this period allows you to avoid the intense heat of summer while enjoying the blooming landscapes. It's an ideal time for outdoor activities and exploring the numerous attractions along Route 66.

Summer (July to Early September): Summer brings warmer temperatures, with some regions experiencing intense heat, particularly in the western sections of Route 66. If you choose to travel during these months, it's advisable to:

- **Vehicle Preparation:** Ensure your vehicle is well-maintained to handle the heat.
- **Hydration:** Carry ample water and stay hydrated.
- **Rest Breaks:** Plan regular stops to rest and avoid fatigue.

Be mindful that summer is also the peak tourist season, leading to busier roads and attractions, as well as higher accommodation rates.

Fall (Late September to October): Early fall provides comfortable temperatures and a decrease in tourist activity. Visiting during this time allows you to experience the route with fewer crowds and pleasant weather, making it easier to explore and enjoy the sights.

Winter (November to March): Winter sees a significant drop in tourism, resulting in fewer crowds and potential off-season rates. However, it's important to consider:

- **Weather Conditions:** Cold temperatures, snow, and ice can lead to road closures, especially in northern and higher elevation areas.
- **Limited Services:** Many attractions, accommodations, and restaurants may be closed or operate on reduced hours during the winter months.

Traveling in winter requires careful planning, including checking road conditions and confirming the availability of services along your intended route.

Packing Essentials

When preparing for your Route 66 road trip, it's important to pack smartly for comfort, safety, and convenience. Here's a list of essentials to make sure you're ready for anything the open road throws your way:

1. **Clothing:**
    - Comfortable clothes for long drives and sightseeing.
    - Layers for changing weather conditions, especially in desert and mountain areas.
    - Comfortable walking shoes for exploring towns and attractions.
    - A hat and sunglasses for sun protection.
    - A light jacket or sweater for cooler evenings.
2. **Roadside Emergency Kit:**
    - Jumper cables, spare tire, and tire-changing tools.
    - Flashlight and extra batteries.
    - First-aid kit with basic medical supplies.
    - Duct tape and basic tools for quick fixes.
3. **Car Essentials:**
    - Car charger for your phone and other electronics.
    - Extra water and snacks in case of long stretches between stops.
    - Gasoline gift cards or cash, especially in more remote areas.
    - Travel insurance and car rental information, if applicable.

4. **Navigation & Travel Aids:**
    - GPS device or a reliable map for navigating the route.
    - Travel apps specific to Route 66 for finding attractions and restaurants.
    - A travel journal or notebook to document your journey.
5. **Personal Items:**
    - Medications and personal hygiene items (toothbrush, deodorant, etc.).
    - Sunscreen and lip balm with SPF.
    - A reusable water bottle to stay hydrated throughout the day.
6. **Tech Gadgets:**
    - Camera to capture the iconic landmarks and roadside attractions.
    - Headphones or earbuds for music or podcasts.
    - A portable power bank for charging devices on the go.
7. **Entertainment for the Road:**
    - Audiobooks, podcasts, or road trip playlists for those long stretches.
8. **Travel Documentation:**
    - Identification (driver's license, passport if needed).
    - Credit cards and cash (in small denominations).
    - Reservation details for accommodations and activities.

Chapter 3: The Complete Route 66 Overview

Key Route 66 States and Cities

Route 66 stretches roughly 2,448 miles, connecting Chicago, Illinois, to Santa Monica, California, and runs through eight states, each with its own unique charm and stories. Here's a snapshot of the key states and the notable cities along the route:

Illinois
- **Chicago:** The journey begins here at the eastern end of Route 66. Known for its vibrant urban life, incredible deep-dish pizza, and rich musical heritage, Chicago sets the stage for the adventure ahead.
- **Springfield:** Steeped in history, this state capital is closely linked to Abraham Lincoln, with sites such as the Lincoln Presidential Library offering a glimpse into the past.

Missouri

- **St. Louis:** Famous for the Gateway Arch, St. Louis blends modern attractions with historical landmarks, providing a lively cultural experience.
- **Joplin:** A charming city that captures the classic spirit of Route 66 with its well-preserved downtown and inviting roadside eateries.

Kansas
- **Galena:** A small town rich in mining history, Galena offers a window into early 20th-century life with its historic architecture and warm, welcoming atmosphere.

Oklahoma
- **Tulsa:** With its art deco buildings and lively music scene, Tulsa adds a touch of modern creativity to the journey.
- **Oklahoma City:** Home to the National Cowboy & Western Heritage Museum, Oklahoma City combines a proud history with contemporary cultural experiences.

Texas
- **Amarillo**: Steeped in cowboy culture, Amarillo is best known for the quirky Cadillac Ranch and a distinctly rugged charm that embodies the spirit of the open road.

New Mexico
- **Albuquerque:** This city offers a blend of Native American and Spanish influences, with its historic Old Town and annual Balloon Fiesta adding a festive air to the trip.
- **Santa Fe:** Renowned for its Pueblo-style architecture and thriving arts scene, Santa Fe provides a creative and historical counterpoint to the route's rugged stretches.

Arizona
- **Flagstaff:** Serving as a gateway to natural wonders like the Grand Canyon, Flagstaff's historic downtown and cooler climate make it a refreshing stop along the journey.
- **Kingman:** Often celebrated as the heart of Route 66, Kingman is filled with museums and vintage attractions that capture the nostalgia of the Mother Road.

California
- **San Bernardino:** Steeped in early Route 66 lore, this city is known for landmarks like the original McDonald's site and offers a deep dive into the road's history.
- **Los Angeles:** A bustling metropolis, LA is a melting pot of cultures and experiences, providing a modern counterbalance to the historic charm of Route 66.
- **Santa Monica:** The journey concludes here at the western terminus of the route, where the iconic Santa Monica Pier welcomes travelers with its ocean views and energy.

Chapter 4: Iconic Stops Along Route 66

Chicago, Illinois

Chicago, known as the "Windy City," is not just the starting point of Route 66—it's a metropolis brimming with history, culture, and world-class attractions. As the third-largest city in the United States, Chicago has something for everyone, from towering skyscrapers to lakeside parks, rich museums to stunning architecture. Whether you're a foodie, art lover, or architecture buff, this city will steal your heart the moment you arrive.

Must-See Attractions in Chicago
1. Millennium Park

- **Description:** Millennium Park is a must-visit when you're in Chicago. The park is home to the famous **Cloud Gate**, better known as "The Bean," which offers perfect photo opportunities with its reflective surface.

- **What to Do:** Walk around the park to enjoy its open spaces, fountains, gardens, and interactive sculptures. If you're there in the summer, you can catch free concerts and movie nights at the **Jay Pritzker Pavilion**.
- **Cost:** Free entry to the park, with special events and performances possibly requiring tickets.
- **Best Time to Visit:** Spring and summer are ideal for enjoying the park's outdoor events and activities.

2. Willis Tower (Formerly Sears Tower)

- **Description:** Standing 1,450 feet tall, Willis Tower is one of Chicago's most iconic buildings. The **Skydeck** on the 103rd floor offers breathtaking panoramic views of the city and Lake Michigan.
- **What to Do:** Don't miss the **Ledge**—glass boxes that extend out from the building, offering a thrilling experience with a view straight down.
- **Cost:** $26 for adults, $18 for children (ages 3-11).
- **Best Time to Visit:** Early mornings or late afternoons for fewer crowds and clearer views.

3. Navy Pier

- **Description:** Located along Lake Michigan, Navy Pier is one of Chicago's top tourist destinations. The pier has a Ferris wheel, boat tours, restaurants, theaters, and shops, making it a family-friendly attraction.
- **What to Do:** Ride the Ferris wheel, explore the **Chicago Children's Museum**, or take a boat tour of the lake. Navy Pier also has seasonal events, like fireworks in the summer.

- **Cost:** Free to walk around; individual attractions (like the Ferris wheel) have separate fees.
- **Best Time to Visit:** Summer for outdoor activities, or during the winter holiday season when the pier is beautifully decorated.

4. The Art Institute of Chicago

- **Description:** One of the oldest and largest art museums in the United States, the Art Institute of Chicago is home to an extensive collection of fine art from around the world.
- **What to Do:** See masterpieces like **Grant Wood's "American Gothic"**, Georges Seurat's **"A Sunday on La Grande Jatte"**, and thousands of other works across multiple galleries.
- **Cost:** $25 for adults, free for children under 14.
- **Best Time to Visit:** Weekdays tend to be less crowded, especially during the spring and fall.

5. The Field Museum

- **Description:** If you're interested in science, history, and natural wonders, The Field Museum should be on your list. It's home to the world-famous **Sue**, the largest and most complete Tyrannosaurus rex fossil ever discovered.
- **What to Do:** Explore exhibits on ancient civilizations, natural history, and the environment. The museum also features rotating special exhibitions.
- **Cost:** $39 for adults, free for children under 2.
- **Best Time to Visit:** Weekdays are less crowded, particularly in the fall and spring.

Where to Stay in Chicago
The Palmer House Hilton

- **Location:** 17 E Monroe St, Chicago, IL 60603

- **Description:** This historic hotel, built in 1871, is a stunning example of classic Chicago architecture. Located in the heart of downtown, it's just steps away from Millennium Park, State Street shopping, and major attractions like the Art Institute of Chicago.
- **What to Expect:** The hotel combines old-world charm with modern amenities, including a fitness center, on-site dining options, and luxurious rooms with views of the city.
- **Cost:** Room rates start at around $150 per night, depending on the season.
- **Best Time to Stay:** Chicago's summer months are popular, but booking in advance ensures you get the best rates and availability.

Where to Eat in Chicago
1. Lou Malnati's Pizzeria

- **Description:** Chicago is famous for its deep-dish pizza, and Lou Malnati's is one of the best places to try it. The buttery crust, gooey cheese, and savory sauce make it a Chicago classic.
- **Cost:** Around $20 for a personal-sized pizza, depending on toppings.
- **What to Do:** Try the **Malnati Chicago Classic**, made with mozzarella, tomato, and a unique sausage blend.
- **Best Time to Visit:** Visit during lunch hours or early evening to avoid long wait times.

2. Portillo's

- **Description:** If you're craving a true Chicago-style hot dog, Portillo's is the place to go. Their famous **Chicago**

dog comes piled high with mustard, relish, onions, tomato, pickles, and sport peppers.
- **Cost:** Hot dogs start around $6, and combo meals are available for $10-$15.
- **What to Do:** Grab a seat, dig into a Chicago-style hot dog, and enjoy the casual vibe of this iconic chain.
- **Best Time to Visit:** Anytime! Portillo's is known for quick service, making it perfect for a casual bite on the go.

Travel Tips for Chicago

- **Getting Around:** Chicago has an excellent public transportation system, including buses and the **L** (elevated train system). It's often the quickest way to get around the city, especially during rush hour.
- **Weather:** Chicago experiences all four seasons, with hot, humid summers and cold, snowy winters. Be sure to check the forecast before your trip and pack accordingly.

St. Louis, Missouri

As you make your way down Route 66, St. Louis is a city that will captivate your senses with its rich history and iconic landmarks. Known as the "Gateway to the West," St. Louis was once the starting point for westward expansion and remains a city full of energy and charm. From the towering Gateway Arch to its lively streets, St. Louis offers something for every traveler.

Must-See Attractions in St. Louis
1. Gateway Arch
- **Description:** Standing 630 feet tall, the Gateway Arch is the tallest man-made monument in the United States, symbolizing the westward expansion of the U.S.
- **What to Do:** Ride the tram to the top for breathtaking panoramic views of St. Louis and the Mississippi River. You can also explore the **Gateway Arch Museum**, which tells the story of the nation's westward journey.
- **Cost:** Tram tickets are $15 for adults, $10 for children (ages 3-15). Museum entry is free.
- **Best Time to Visit:** The Arch is open year-round, but the best time to visit is in spring or fall, when the weather is mild and the views are clear.

2. St. Louis Zoo

- **Description:** The St. Louis Zoo is one of the best in the country, and it's completely free to visit! Home to over 12,000 animals, the zoo spans 90 acres in **Forest Park**.
- **What to Do:** Explore the many animal exhibits, including big cats, elephants, penguins, and the famous **River's Edge** area, which features animals from Africa.
- **Cost:** Free entry. Certain attractions, like the **Wildly Wild** rides, may have additional costs.

- **Best Time to Visit:** The zoo is open year-round, but spring and summer are the best times to see the animals at their most active.

3. The Missouri Botanical Garden

- **Description:** A 79-acre botanical garden featuring stunning landscapes, plant collections, and historical architecture. It's a peaceful place to relax and explore nature.
- **What to Do:** Stroll through the Japanese Garden, check out the **Climatron**—a geodesic dome housing tropical plants—and visit the historic **Henry Shaw Garden**.
- **Cost:** $14 for adults, $6 for children (ages 3-12).
- **Best Time to Visit:** Spring is perfect for seeing the garden in full bloom, but it's beautiful year-round.

4. The National Blues Museum

- **Description:** As the birthplace of blues music, St. Louis has a rich musical legacy. The **National Blues Museum** celebrates the culture, history, and artists that shaped this iconic genre.
- **What to Do:** Explore exhibits on the evolution of blues music, featuring legendary artists like **B.B. King** and **Chuck Berry**, and immerse yourself in the soulful sound of this American music style.
- **Cost:** $15 for adults, $10 for children (ages 6-18).
- **Best Time to Visit:** The museum is open year-round, but if you visit in April, you can catch the annual **St. Louis Blues Week**.

5. City Museum

- **Description:** The **City Museum** is an eccentric, interactive museum housed in a former shoe factory. It's unlike any other museum you've ever visited!
- **What to Do:** Wander through the maze-like exhibits, climb up a giant indoor slide, explore caves, or go on the rooftop for a bird's-eye view of the city. It's a perfect stop for families or anyone looking for a little adventure.
- **Cost:** $14 for adults, $8 for children (ages 3-12).
- **Best Time to Visit:** Weekdays are less crowded, especially if you're traveling with kids.

Where to Stay in St. Louis
The Chase Park Plaza Royal Sonesta

The Chase Park Plaza Royal Sonesta

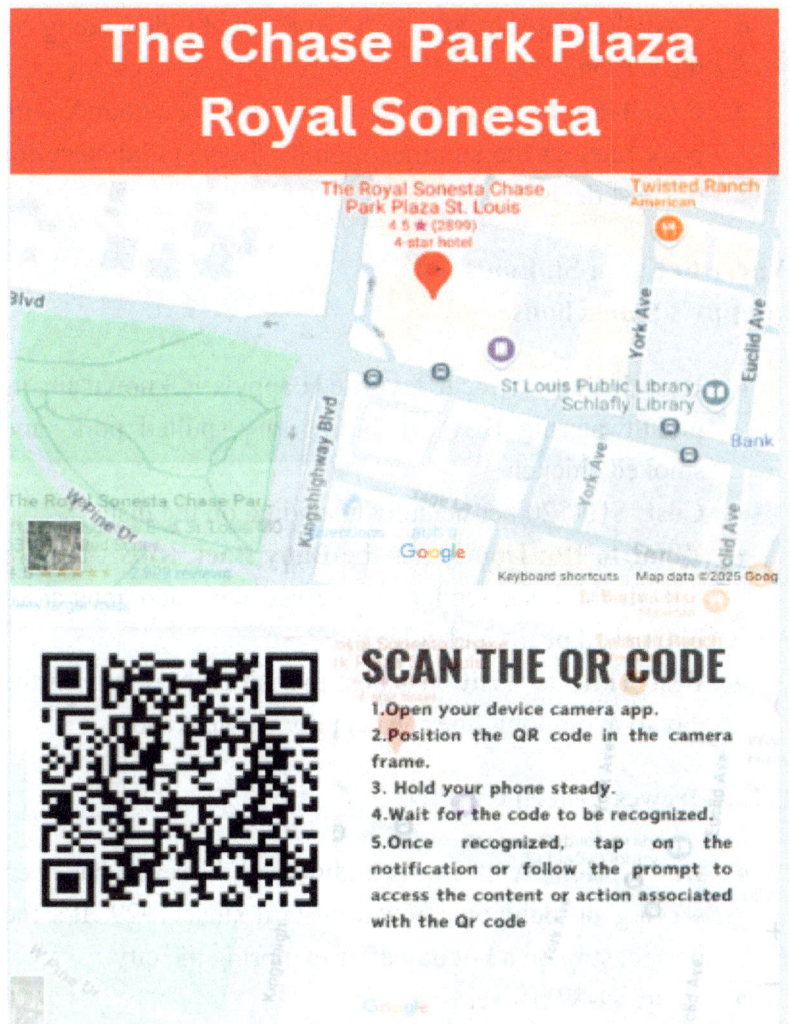

- **Location:** 212 N Kingshighway Blvd, St. Louis, MO 63108
- **Description:** A historic luxury hotel in the heart of St. Louis, located near **Forest Park** and just a short drive from the Gateway Arch. The hotel features elegant rooms, an outdoor pool, and a great dining option, **The Tenderloin Room**.

- **Cost:** Rooms start around $150 per night, depending on the season.
- **Best Time to Stay:** The hotel is open year-round, with peak rates in the summer months. Book in advance for the best deals.

Where to Eat in St. Louis
1. Pappy's Smokehouse

- **Description:** A local favorite, Pappy's is known for its mouthwatering BBQ, including ribs, pulled pork, and smoked chicken.
- **Cost:** $10-$20 per person, depending on the dish.
- **What to Do:** Don't miss the **Baby Back Ribs**—they're fall-off-the-bone tender and served with delicious sides like baked beans and coleslaw.
- **Best Time to Visit:** It's best to visit early or late in the day to avoid long lines, especially on weekends.

2. Ted Drewes Frozen Custard

- **Description:** A St. Louis tradition, Ted Drewes has been serving up delicious frozen custard since 1929. It's the perfect stop on a hot day after exploring the city.
- **Cost:** $4-$7 per serving.
- **What to Do:** Try the **Concretes**, a thick custard blended with your choice of mix-ins. The **"Gooey Butter Cake"** concrete is a popular choice.
- **Best Time to Visit:** Ted Drewes is open year-round, but it's especially popular in summer.

Travel Tips for St. Louis

- **Getting Around:** St. Louis is easy to explore by car, but downtown also has a free trolley service that runs along the main attractions.
- **Weather:** Summers can be hot and humid, so pack light, breathable clothing. Winters are cold and can be snowy, so make sure to dress warmly if visiting during the winter months.

Tulsa, Oklahoma

Nestled in the heart of the American Midwest, Tulsa offers a mix of rich history, arts, and modern energy. Once known as the "Oil Capital of the World," Tulsa is full of character, with its stunning art deco architecture, lively cultural scene, and deep connection to Route 66. This city's friendly atmosphere and unique charm make it a must-visit stop along your Route 66 adventure.

Must-See Attractions in Tulsa
1. Art Deco Architecture

- **Description:** Tulsa boasts one of the country's best collections of art deco architecture, a legacy from the city's boom in the early 20th century.
- **What to Do:** Take a walking tour of the **Art Deco District**, which includes iconic buildings like the **Boston Avenue Methodist Church** and the **Philcade Building**. Stop by the **Tulsa Union Depot**, an architectural gem from the 1930s.
- **Cost:** Free to walk around, though some buildings may charge for tours.
- **Best Time to Visit:** Spring and fall are ideal for walking tours, with comfortable temperatures and beautiful cityscapes.

2. Route 66 Historic District

- **Description:** Tulsa is a key stop along Route 66, offering a variety of classic diners, old motels, and quirky attractions.
- **What to Do:** Drive down the **Route 66 Historic District**, where you can see vintage motels, roadside signs, and cafes that take you back in time. Don't miss the famous **Blue Dome District**, a lively area with shops, bars, and restaurants.
- **Cost:** Free to drive through the district; dining and shopping are extra.
- **Best Time to Visit:** The spring and fall months offer pleasant temperatures for exploring the historic district.

3. Tulsa's Philbrook Museum of Art

- **Description:** Housed in an Italianate villa, the **Philbrook Museum** is one of the premier art institutions

in Oklahoma, featuring impressive collections of American and European art.
- **What to Do:** Wander through the museum's galleries, and take in beautiful works from artists like **John Singer Sargent** and **Georgia O'Keeffe**. The gardens surrounding the museum are also worth exploring, offering peace and tranquility.
- **Cost:** $12 for adults, free for children under 18.
- **Best Time to Visit:** Weekdays are less crowded, and spring brings blooming flowers in the gardens.

4. The Golden Driller

- **Description:** One of the world's largest freestanding statues, the **Golden Driller** stands 75 feet tall and celebrates Tulsa's history in the oil industry.
- **What to Do:** Take a photo with the Golden Driller and learn about the history of the oil boom that helped shape the city. You'll find this iconic statue at the **Tulsa State Fairgrounds**, an easy stop while you're in the city.
- **Cost:** Free.
- **Best Time to Visit:** Any time of the year, but the fairgrounds are busiest during the **Tulsa State Fair** in the fall.

5. Tulsa Zoo

- **Description:** The **Tulsa Zoo** is home to more than 1,500 animals and is a fantastic stop for families or animal lovers.
- **What to Do:** Visit the **African Savannah** to see lions, giraffes, and elephants, or explore the **Wildlife Trek** exhibit, featuring animals from North America. The zoo

35

is also known for its hands-on exhibits and beautiful grounds.
- **Cost:** $10 for adults, $6 for children (ages 3-11).
- **Best Time to Visit:** Spring and summer are perfect for seeing the animals at their most active.

Where to Stay in Tulsa
The Mayo Hotel

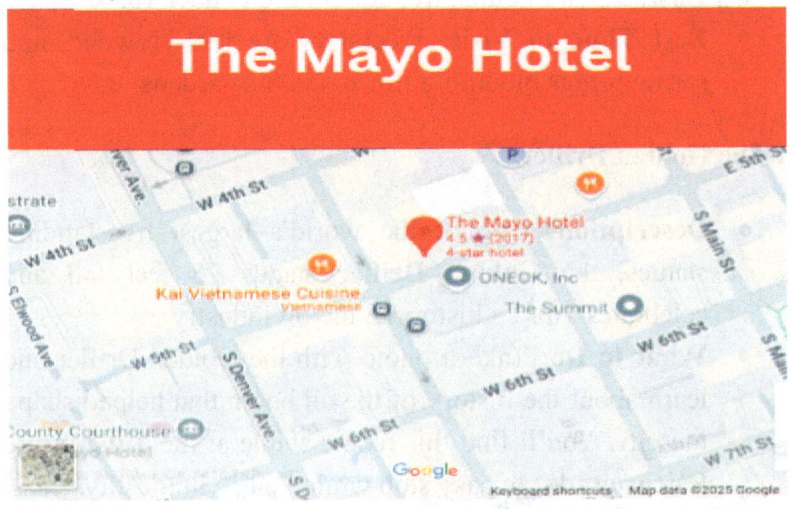

SCAN THE QR CODE
1. Open your device camera app.
2. Position the QR code in the camera frame.
3. Hold your phone steady.
4. Wait for the code to be recognized.
5. Once recognized, tap on the notification or follow the prompt to access the content or action associated with the Qr code

- **Location:** 115 W 5th St, Tulsa, OK 74103

- **Description:** A historic landmark, the **Mayo Hotel** combines classic charm with modern luxury. Once the tallest building in Oklahoma, this hotel offers stunning views of downtown Tulsa and is an excellent spot for those looking for elegance.
- **What to Expect:** Spacious rooms, a rooftop bar, and a prime location near attractions like the Tulsa Performing Arts Center and Route 66 Historic District.
- **Cost:** Rooms start around $150 per night, depending on the season.
- **Best Time to Stay:** The hotel is open year-round, but booking in advance can help you secure the best rates, especially during busy seasons.

Where to Eat in Tulsa
1. Pappadeaux's Seafood Kitchen

- **Description:** A local favorite for seafood lovers, **Pappadeaux's** serves up fresh, flavorful dishes inspired by Cajun and Creole cuisines.
- **Cost:** Most main courses range from $15-$30.
- **What to Do:** Try their **Cajun Crawfish** or **Blackened Redfish** for a true taste of southern flavors.
- **Best Time to Visit:** Early evening or weekdays to avoid peak crowds.

2. The Brook Restaurant and Bar

- **Description:** A staple in Tulsa, **The Brook** is a casual spot known for its hearty pub fare and friendly atmosphere.
- **Cost:** Entrees range from $10-$20.

- **What to Do:** Enjoy their famous **Brook Burger** or try a classic **fish and chips**.
- **Best Time to Visit:** Lunch and early dinner hours are perfect for avoiding the evening rush.

Travel Tips for Tulsa

- **Getting Around:** Tulsa is easy to navigate by car, and most attractions are within a short drive of each other. Consider renting a bike for a more leisurely exploration of the Route 66 Historic District.
- **Weather:** Summers in Tulsa can be hot, with temperatures often reaching the 90s°F (30°C). Fall and spring offer milder temperatures, making them the best times to visit.

Amarillo, Texas

Nestled in the heart of the Texas Panhandle, Amarillo is a quintessential stop on your Route 66 adventure. Known for its cowboy spirit, wide-open spaces, and a rich history tied to the American West, Amarillo is a place where the past meets the present in a big way.

Must-See Attractions in Amarillo

1. Cadillac Ranch

- **Description:** Cadillac Ranch is one of the most famous roadside attractions along Route 66. This art installation features 10 half-buried Cadillacs, each buried nose-first in the ground. It's a striking and colorful tribute to the evolution of the Cadillac tailfin design, a symbol of the car culture that made Route 66 legendary.
- **What to Do:** The fun part is that visitors are encouraged to spray paint the cars. Bring your own cans of spray paint to add your mark to the artwork, or just snap a photo with this quirky and iconic display.
- **Cost:** Free to visit.
- **Best Time to Visit:** The best time to visit is during the cooler months, spring or fall, as Texas summers can be extremely hot.
- **Website:** N/A – this is an open-air art installation with no admission fees.

2. The Big Texan Steak Ranch

- **Description:** A legendary spot for steak lovers, the Big Texan is famous for its 72-ounce steak challenge. The restaurant serves hearty portions of steaks, ribs, and other Texas BBQ favorites in a cowboy-themed atmosphere.
- **What to Do:** If you're up for a challenge, try to conquer the famous **72-ounce steak**. If you finish the entire meal (steak, salad, shrimp cocktail, baked potato, and bread), it's free! Even if you don't take on the challenge, the regular menu offers classic Texan eats.
- **Cost:** Prices vary by meal, but the 72-ounce steak challenge is free if you can finish it.

- **Best Time to Visit:** The Big Texan is open year-round, though it can get crowded during peak meal times.
- **Website:** Big Texan Steak Ranch

3. Amarillo Route 66 Historic District

- **Description:** Amarillo's Route 66 Historic District offers a nostalgic look at the city's Route 66 heritage. This district is full of vintage motels, retro diners, and classic roadside signs that will take you back to the golden age of the highway.
- **What to Do:** Walk through the district and explore the vintage shops, stop by local diners, and admire the old-school architecture. Don't forget to visit the **Route 66 Texas Visitors Center**, where you can grab maps and learn more about the history of the Mother Road in Amarillo.
- **Cost:** Free to explore, but bring cash for shopping or dining.
- **Best Time to Visit:** Spring and fall offer comfortable temperatures for a leisurely stroll through the district.

4. The American Quarter Horse Hall of Fame & Museum

- **Description:** Amarillo has a strong connection to the cowboy and rodeo culture, and the **American Quarter Horse Hall of Fame & Museum** is a tribute to the horse breed that helped shape the American West.
- **What to Do:** Learn about the history of the American Quarter Horse, see exhibits on famous horses and riders, and explore the museum's interactive displays.
- **Cost:** $8 for adults, $5 for children (ages 5-12).

- **Best Time to Visit:** The museum is open year-round, but check their website for special events or exhibits during your visit.
- **Website:** American Quarter Horse Hall of Fame

5. Palo Duro Canyon State Park

- **Description:** Known as the "Grand Canyon of Texas," **Palo Duro Canyon** is one of the most scenic spots in the state. With its dramatic red rock formations, sweeping views, and abundant wildlife, this state park is a must-see for nature lovers and hikers.
- **What to Do:** Explore the park's hiking trails, including the **Lighthouse Trail**, which takes you to the park's most famous landmark. The park also offers opportunities for camping, horseback riding, and stargazing.
- **Cost:** Entrance fee is $8 per vehicle.
- **Best Time to Visit:** Spring and fall offer the best weather for outdoor activities, with milder temperatures and clear skies.
- **Website:** Palo Duro Canyon State Park

Where to Stay in Amarillo
The Historic Route 66 Inn

The Historic Route 66 Inn

SCAN THE QR CODE

1. Open your device camera app.
2. Position the QR code in the camera frame.
3. Hold your phone steady.
4. Wait for the code to be recognized.
5. Once recognized, tap on the notification or follow the prompt to access the content or action associated with the Qr code

- **Location:** 2218 E. I-40, Amarillo, TX 79104

- **Description:** A classic roadside motel that perfectly fits the Route 66 vibe, offering cozy rooms with modern amenities at an affordable price.
- **What to Expect:** Stay in a retro-themed room with vintage furnishings, and enjoy the convenience of being close to major Route 66 attractions like Cadillac Ranch and the Historic District.
- **Cost:** Rates start around $60 per night, depending on the season.
- **Best Time to Stay:** Amarillo is a year-round destination, but spring and fall are ideal for comfortable weather and fewer tourists.

Where to Eat in Amarillo
The Golden Light Cafe

- **Description:** Known as Amarillo's oldest bar and grill, **The Golden Light Cafe** has been serving up Tex-Mex, burgers, and cold beer since 1946. It's a Route 66 favorite for locals and travelers alike.
- **Cost:** Meals range from $5 for a burger to $12 for a full entrée.
- **What to Do:** Try the famous **Golden Light Burger**, paired with their signature homemade fries. It's a casual spot with a lot of character.
- **Best Time to Visit:** It's busiest during lunch and dinner hours, so arrive early or late to avoid the crowd.

Travel Tips for Amarillo

- **Getting Around:** Amarillo is easy to explore by car, and many of the major Route 66 attractions are within a short drive of each other.

- **Weather:** Summers can be hot, with temperatures often climbing above 100°F (38°C), so be prepared with sunscreen, water, and a hat. The spring and fall seasons offer milder temperatures, making them the best times to visit.

Albuquerque, New Mexico

Albuquerque, with its blend of Native American, Hispanic, and Anglo cultures, is one of the most lively stops along Route 66. Nestled in the high desert and surrounded by dramatic mountains, this city is rich in history, art, and natural beauty.

Must-See Attractions in Albuquerque
1. Old Town Albuquerque

- **Description:** Old Town is the heart of Albuquerque, where history and modern-day culture collide. The area is lined with adobe-style buildings, cobblestone streets, and a variety of shops, galleries, and restaurants.
- **What to Do:** Visit the **San Felipe de Neri Church**, which dates back to 1793, explore the **New Mexico Museum of Natural History & Science**, or browse

through local shops offering Native American art and jewelry.
- **Cost:** Free to explore, though individual attractions may have their own admission fees.
- **Best Time to Visit:** Spring and fall are perfect for walking around Old Town, with mild temperatures and fewer tourists.

2. The Albuquerque International Balloon Fiesta

- **Description:** The **Albuquerque International Balloon Fiesta** is one of the largest and most photographed ballooning events in the world. Held annually in October, the event features hundreds of hot air balloons soaring over the city's desert landscape at sunrise.
- **What to Do:** Watch the stunning mass ascensions, attend ballooning workshops, or take a balloon ride for an unforgettable view of the city.
- **Cost:** Admission to the event is $10 for adults and $5 for children. Balloon rides have additional costs, typically around $200 per person.
- **Best Time to Visit:** October, during the Balloon Fiesta, is the best time to visit Albuquerque for this amazing spectacle.
- **Website:** Albuquerque International Balloon Fiesta

3. Route 66 Historic District

- **Description:** Albuquerque's Route 66 Historic District is a treasure trove of vintage motels, neon signs, diners, and quirky roadside attractions.
- **What to Do:** Stroll down **Central Avenue**, which once was part of the iconic Route 66. Stop by the **Route 66**

Diner for a nostalgic meal, or check out the **KiMo Theatre**, a beautifully restored 1920s building with Native American-inspired art deco design.
- **Cost:** Free to walk around the district; dining and shopping are extra.
- **Best Time to Visit:** Spring and fall offer the best weather for exploring the district.

4. Sandia Peak Tramway

- **Description:** For a panoramic view of Albuquerque and the surrounding desert, hop on the **Sandia Peak Tramway**. The tram ride takes you up to the top of **Sandia Mountain**, where you'll be treated to breathtaking vistas.
- **What to Do:** Enjoy a scenic ride to the top, where you can hike, dine at the **Sandia Peak Tramway Restaurant**, or simply take in the incredible views.
- **Cost:** $25 for adults, $12 for children (ages 5-12).
- **Best Time to Visit:** The tram operates year-round, but spring and fall provide the best views and mild temperatures.
- **Website:** Sandia Peak Tramway

5. Indian Pueblo Cultural Center

- **Description:** The **Indian Pueblo Cultural Center** offers visitors the opportunity to learn about the history, art, and culture of New Mexico's 19 Native American pueblos.
- **What to Do:** Explore exhibits on traditional Native American art, pottery, and beadwork, and learn about the

history of the pueblos. The center also offers live performances and demonstrations.
- **Cost:** $8 for adults, $5 for children (ages 5-12).
- **Best Time to Visit:** The center is open year-round, but if you visit in summer, you can also enjoy the cultural events and performances.
- **Website:** Indian Pueblo Cultural Center

Where to Stay in Albuquerque
Hotel Albuquerque at Old Town

SCAN THE QR CODE
1. Open your device camera app.
2. Position the QR code in the camera frame.
3. Hold your phone steady.
4. Wait for the code to be recognized.
5. Once recognized, tap on the notification or follow the prompt to access the content or action associated with the Qr code

- **Location:** 800 Rio Grande Blvd NW, Albuquerque, NM 87104
- **Description:** A beautiful hotel located just a short walk from Old Town, the **Hotel Albuquerque at Old Town** combines Southwestern charm with modern amenities. The hotel features a stunning courtyard, a restaurant serving New Mexican cuisine, and a pool.
- **What to Expect:** Cozy, culturally-themed rooms with views of the Sandia Mountains, as well as an on-site spa and several dining options.
- **Cost:** Rooms start at around $120 per night, depending on the season.
- **Best Time to Stay:** The hotel is open year-round, with peak rates in summer and fall. It's especially nice to stay here during the Albuquerque Balloon Fiesta for easy access to the event.

Where to Eat in Albuquerque
1. The Route 66 Diner

- **Description:** A classic Route 66 diner serving up breakfast, lunch, and dinner in a retro setting. The **Route 66 Diner** offers a taste of Americana with everything from milkshakes to burgers and fries.
- **Cost:** $10-$15 per meal.
- **What to Do:** Try the **Green Chile Cheeseburger** or the **Fried Chicken Tenders**—two local favorites.
- **Best Time to Visit:** Open year-round, but it's particularly fun to visit during breakfast when you can enjoy the diner's old-school atmosphere.

2. El Pinto Restaurant and Cantina

- **Description:** A long-time Albuquerque favorite, **El Pinto** serves traditional New Mexican dishes like enchiladas, tamales, and sopapillas, all made with locally sourced ingredients.
- **Cost:** $12-$25 per entrée.
- **What to Do:** Try the **El Pinto Burrito** or the **Carnitas Tacos** for an authentic taste of New Mexico.
- **Best Time to Visit:** El Pinto is a popular spot, so consider making a reservation for dinner, especially on weekends.

Travel Tips

- **Getting Around:** Albuquerque is easy to navigate by car, and many of the attractions are within a short drive of each other. The city also has a **bus system** that makes it convenient for travelers to get around.
- **Weather:** The weather in Albuquerque can be hot in the summer, with temperatures reaching over 90°F (32°C), so make sure to bring sunscreen, a hat, and plenty of water. Spring and fall are the best times to visit, offering mild temperatures and clear skies.

Flagstaff, Arizona

Located in the heart of northern Arizona, Flagstaff is a scenic gem and a must-visit stop on your Route 66 journey. With its picturesque mountain views, rich history, and a perfect blend of outdoor adventure and small-town charm, Flagstaff is a place where you can unwind, explore, and connect with the American Southwest. The city's historic downtown area, arts scene, and proximity to natural wonders make it an ideal spot for those looking to add a bit of outdoor magic to their road trip.

Must-See Attractions in Flagstaff
1. Route 66 Historic District

- **Description:** The heart of Flagstaff's Route 66 heritage lies in its historic downtown district. This area is full of charming brick buildings, unique shops, local cafes, and Route 66 memorabilia.
- **What to Do:** Walk the streets lined with vintage signs, visit the **Historic Weatherford Hotel**, and stop by the **Flagstaff Visitor Center** to learn about the city's Route 66 legacy. Don't forget to check out the quirky local

shops for souvenirs or grab a bite at one of the many Route 66 diners.
- **Cost:** Free to explore; meals and shopping costs vary.
- **Best Time to Visit:** Spring and fall are ideal, with cooler temperatures perfect for strolling around the district.

2. Lowell Observatory

- **Description:** For those fascinated by the stars, the **Lowell Observatory** is a must-visit. This historic site is where **Pluto** was discovered in 1930 and offers some of the best stargazing in the country.
- **What to Do:** Take a guided tour of the observatory, attend a public stargazing session, or learn about the history of space exploration at one of the many interactive exhibits.
- **Cost:** $10 for adults, $5 for children (ages 5-17).
- **Best Time to Visit:** The observatory is open year-round, but the best time for stargazing is in the summer, when the skies are clearer and the temperatures are warmer.
- **Website:** Lowell Observatory

3. Walnut Canyon National Monument

- **Description:** About 10 miles from Flagstaff, **Walnut Canyon** offers a unique glimpse into the past. The monument features ancient **cliff dwellings** that were once home to the Sinagua people, who lived in the area around 1,000 years ago.
- **What to Do:** Take the **Island Trail** to explore the cliff dwellings, walk through the narrow canyon, and enjoy stunning views of the canyon and surrounding pine forests.

- **Cost:** $10 per vehicle for entrance.
- **Best Time to Visit:** Spring and fall are the best times to visit when the weather is mild, and the trails are less crowded.
- **Website:** Walnut Canyon National Monument

4. Grand Canyon National Park

- **Description:** Flagstaff is just an hour and a half south of one of the world's most famous natural wonders: the **Grand Canyon**. Whether you're exploring the South Rim or hiking down into the canyon itself, the views are simply breathtaking.
- **What to Do:** Visit the South Rim for stunning panoramic views, take a helicopter tour for an aerial perspective, or hike one of the many trails for an up-close experience with the canyon's beauty.
- **Cost:** $35 for a 7-day vehicle pass to the park.
- **Best Time to Visit:** Late spring to early fall offers the best weather for outdoor activities and less risk of snow or ice.
- **Website:** Grand Canyon National Park

5. Arizona Snowbowl

- **Description:** While Flagstaff is known for its warm, sunny days, it also boasts some of the best skiing and snowboarding in Arizona. The **Arizona Snowbowl** is located just outside of the city, offering winter sports enthusiasts a fun escape into the mountains.
- **What to Do:** Ski, snowboard, or take a scenic ride up the chairlift to enjoy panoramic views of Flagstaff and

the surrounding forest. In the summer months, you can hike and enjoy the cooler mountain air.
- **Cost:** Lift tickets vary from $60 to $100, depending on the season and time of day.
- **Best Time to Visit:** Winter for skiing and snowboarding, or summer for hiking and outdoor activities.
- **Website:** Arizona Snowbowl

Where to Stay in Flagstaff
1. Hotel Monte Vista

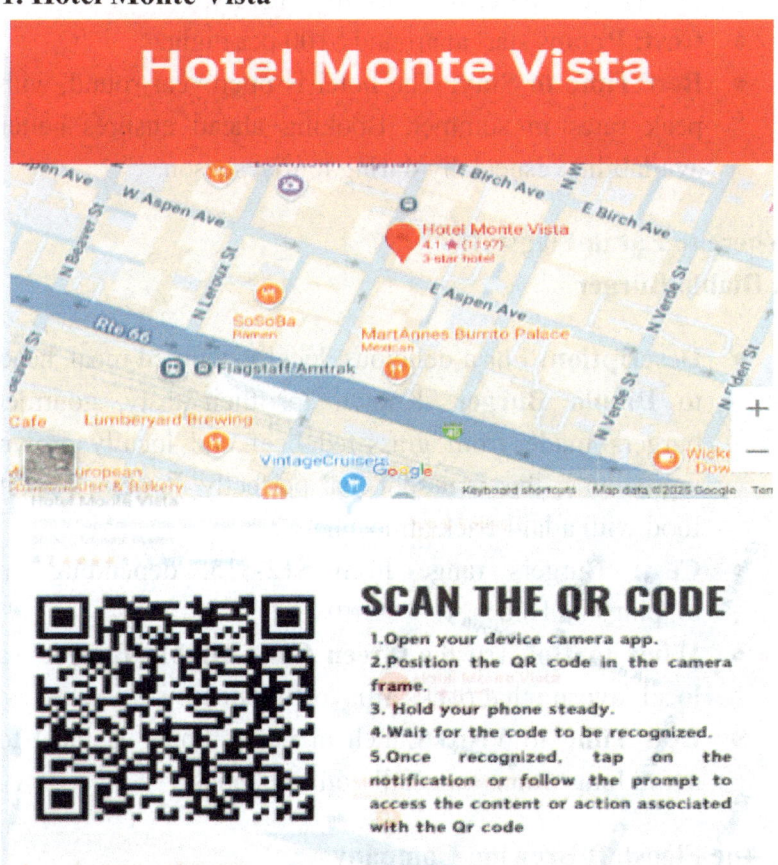

Hotel Monte Vista

SCAN THE QR CODE
1. Open your device camera app.
2. Position the QR code in the camera frame.
3. Hold your phone steady.
4. Wait for the code to be recognized.
5. Once recognized, tap on the notification or follow the prompt to access the content or action associated with the Qr code

- **Location:** 100 N San Francisco St, Flagstaff, AZ 86001
- **Description:** A historic hotel that has been an icon of Flagstaff since 1927, **Hotel Monte Vista** offers old-world charm combined with modern amenities. Situated right in the heart of downtown, it's a perfect base for exploring Flagstaff's Route 66 district and nearby attractions.
- **What to Expect:** Cozy rooms with vintage charm, a lively bar, and a historic atmosphere. It's not just a place to stay, but a piece of Flagstaff's history.
- **Cost:** Rooms start at around $100 per night.
- **Best Time to Stay:** The hotel is open year-round, with peak rates in summer. Booking ahead ensures better availability, especially during tourist season.

Where to Eat in Flagstaff
1. Diablo Burger

- **Description:** For a delicious, locally-sourced meal, head to **Diablo Burger**. Known for their tasty, gourmet burgers made from grass-fed beef and locally grown ingredients, this is a spot that perfectly combines great food with a laid-back atmosphere.
- **Cost:** Burgers range from $12-$15, depending on toppings and sides.
- **What to Do:** Try the **Green Chile Diablo Burger**—a local favorite that packs a flavorful punch.
- **Best Time to Visit:** Lunch or early dinner is ideal to avoid long waits, especially on weekends.

2. The Flagstaff Brewing Company

- **Description:** If you're a craft beer enthusiast, **Flagstaff Brewing Company** is a must-visit. Serving a variety of locally brewed beers, the brewery offers a relaxed atmosphere perfect for enjoying a cold drink after a day of sightseeing.
- **Cost:** Beer prices range from $5-$7 per pint, and pub fare such as burgers and fries are around $10-$15.
- **What to Do:** Enjoy a fresh brew like the **Flagstaff IPA** or **Route 66 Red** while relaxing in the cozy, pub-like setting.
- **Best Time to Visit:** Visit in the late afternoon or early evening to unwind with a drink before heading out for dinner.

Travel Tips for Flagstaff

- **Getting Around:** Flagstaff is a small city, and most of the attractions are within a short drive or walk from each other. The downtown area is walkable, making it easy to explore on foot.
- **Weather:** Flagstaff's high elevation means it enjoys cooler temperatures than much of Arizona, making it perfect for hiking in the summer and skiing in the winter. Winter temperatures can drop significantly, so pack accordingly if you're visiting in colder months.

Santa Monica, California

The journey along Route 66 concludes in Santa Monica, California, where the iconic pier marks the end of this historic road. Known for its beautiful beaches, iconic landmarks, and vibrant atmosphere, Santa Monica offers a perfect blend of fun, relaxation, and coastal beauty. Whether you're looking to soak in the sun on the beach, enjoy some shopping, or simply stroll through the historic pier, Santa Monica will leave you with memories of your Route 66 adventure that you'll never forget.

Must-See Attractions in Santa Monica
1. Santa Monica Pier

- **Description:** The Santa Monica Pier, with its Ferris wheel, roller coaster, and aquarium, is one of the most recognizable symbols of California's coastline. It has been a part of the city since 1909 and remains a popular spot for tourists and locals alike.
- **What to Do:** Ride the solar-powered **Pacific Wheel** Ferris wheel for stunning ocean views, explore the **Santa Monica Pier Aquarium**, or enjoy the arcade and restaurants along the pier.

- **Cost:** The pier is free to visit, but individual attractions (like the Ferris wheel) have their own fees—$5 per ride.
- **Best Time to Visit:** The pier is open year-round, but weekdays, especially in the early morning or late afternoon, are the best times to avoid the crowds.
- **Website:** Santa Monica Pier

2. Third Street Promenade

- **Description:** A pedestrian-only street, the **Third Street Promenade** is one of Santa Monica's most famous shopping and dining destinations. Lined with boutiques, department stores, street performers, and restaurants, it offers something for everyone.
- **What to Do:** Shop at high-end boutiques or trendy stores, enjoy live performances by street artists, and dine at one of the many cafes or restaurants that line the promenade.
- **Cost:** Free to explore; shopping and dining costs vary.
- **Best Time to Visit:** It's best to visit during the afternoon or evening when the promenade is bustling with activity. The area is especially vibrant during weekends.

3. Palisades Park

- **Description:** Offering sweeping views of the Pacific Ocean, **Palisades Park** is one of the best spots in Santa Monica for a scenic stroll. The park stretches along the cliffs, providing beautiful walking paths, gardens, and peaceful spots to relax.
- **What to Do:** Take a leisurely walk along the park's paths, relax by the ocean, or watch the sunset over the Pacific. The park is also home to the famous

International Chess Park, where visitors can enjoy a game of chess.
- **Cost:** Free to visit.
- **Best Time to Visit:** Early morning or late afternoon for a peaceful experience and the best views of the ocean.

4. Venice Beach

- **Description:** Just a short drive from Santa Monica, **Venice Beach** offers a more eclectic and laid-back vibe. Known for its funky boardwalk, street performers, muscle beach gym, and vibrant skate park, Venice is the place to experience California's free-spirited culture.
- **What to Do:** Rent a bike and cruise along the beach path, visit the **Venice Skate Park**, or just people-watch on the boardwalk. If you're into unique shopping, check out the quirky shops and art galleries.
- **Cost:** Free to visit; bike rentals typically cost around $10-$20 per hour.
- **Best Time to Visit:** The best time to visit is in the early morning to avoid the crowds, or late afternoon for a beautiful sunset along the beach.

5. The Annenberg Community Beach House

- **Description:** Once the private estate of William Randolph Hearst, the **Annenberg Community Beach House** is now a public space that offers a variety of activities. Located at the edge of the beach, it features a historic pool, a café, and access to the beach.
- **What to Do:** Swim in the historic pool, relax by the beach, or enjoy a meal at the café. The **Beach House** also offers seasonal programs and events.

- **Cost:** Free to visit the beach; pool access is $10 for adults and $4 for children.
- **Best Time to Visit:** Summer is ideal for enjoying the pool and the beach, but the Beach House is open year-round.

Where to Stay in Santa Monica
Shutters on the Beach

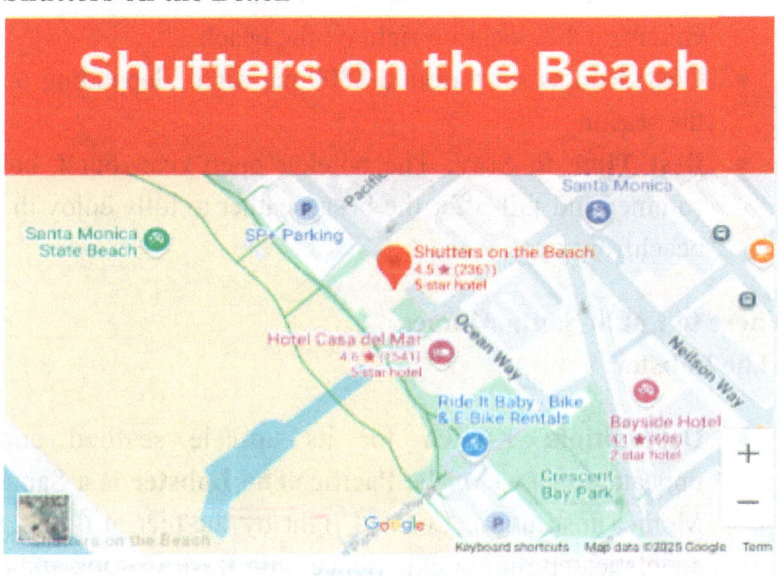

Shutters on the Beach

SCAN THE QR CODE
1. Open your device camera app.
2. Position the QR code in the camera frame.
3. Hold your phone steady.
4. Wait for the code to be recognized.
5. Once recognized, tap on the notification or follow the prompt to access the content or action associated with the Qr code

- **Location:** 1 Pico Blvd, Santa Monica, CA 90405
- **Description:** A luxurious beachfront hotel that offers stunning ocean views and top-notch amenities, **Shutters on the Beach** is the perfect place to relax and enjoy the beauty of the California coast.
- **What to Expect:** Rooms with elegant, beach-inspired decor, a heated outdoor pool, spa services, and an on-site restaurant with ocean views. It's a luxurious escape with an unbeatable location right on the beach.
- **Cost:** Rooms start around $500 per night, depending on the season.
- **Best Time to Stay:** The hotel is open year-round, but summer and fall offer the best weather to fully enjoy the beachfront experience.

Where to Eat in Santa Monica
1. The Lobster

- **Description:** Known for its upscale seafood and unbeatable views of the Pacific, **The Lobster** is a Santa Monica institution. Located right by the pier, it offers a sophisticated dining experience with fresh seafood and a relaxed ambiance.
- **Cost:** Entrees range from $30 to $50, depending on the dish.
- **What to Do:** Try their signature lobster dishes or enjoy fresh oysters while watching the sunset over the ocean.
- **Best Time to Visit:** For the best experience, visit around sunset, when you can enjoy stunning views along with a delicious meal.

2. Huckleberry Café & Bakery

- **Description:** A charming café with a focus on fresh, organic ingredients, **Huckleberry** is a great spot for breakfast or brunch in Santa Monica. The menu features homemade pastries, healthy breakfast bowls, and artisan sandwiches.
- **Cost:** Breakfast and brunch options range from $10 to $20.
- **What to Do:** Try the **Brioche French Toast** or the **Avocado Toast** for a fresh, satisfying meal.
- **Best Time to Visit:** Breakfast and brunch hours are busy, but it's worth the wait. Try to visit during off-peak times for a quieter experience.

Travel Tips

- **Getting Around:** Santa Monica is very walkable, and many attractions are within a short distance from each other. For longer trips, rent a bike or use public transportation, including the **Big Blue Bus** system.
- **Weather:** Santa Monica enjoys mild, pleasant weather year-round, with temperatures ranging from the mid-60s to mid-70s°F (18-24°C). Summers can be cooler than inland areas due to the ocean breeze, making it a perfect beach getaway.

Chapter 6: Local Culture and Traditions

Small-Town America

What makes small towns along Route 66 so appealing? It's the warmth of the people, the quiet rhythm of everyday life, and the way the past and present coexist so naturally. In these towns, you'll find welcoming locals who are eager to share their stories, small shops filled with treasures, and streets lined with history. Small towns are often defined by their sense of community, where everyone knows each other, and you feel like part of the family—even if you're just passing through.

Unique Traditions And Festivals

Small towns along Route 66 are full of unique traditions that reflect the values and history of the area. These festivals, parades, and community events are what give these places their character and provide a glimpse into the cultural heart of the region.

- **Local Festivals:** Whether it's a chili cook-off, a classic car show, or a music festival, many small towns along

Route 66 host annual events that bring the community together. These celebrations are an excellent opportunity to experience local culture, meet the people, and enjoy some delicious regional food. These events often showcase the town's history, pride, and creativity, giving you an authentic taste of local life.

- **Holiday Traditions:** Small towns often go all out during holidays like Christmas and the 4th of July, with festive parades, light displays, and family-friendly events. These celebrations are more intimate than in big cities, offering a closer connection to the community and a chance to see how small-town America honors its traditions.

Family-Owned Shops and Eateries

One of the best ways to experience the charm of small-town America is by visiting the local shops and eateries. These small businesses are often the lifeblood of a town, providing unique goods and services that reflect the town's culture and history. Many of these businesses have been passed down through generations, preserving the values and traditions of their founders.

- **Local Diners and Cafes:** Step into a local diner or cafe, and you'll find a warm welcome, classic comfort food, and an atmosphere that feels like home. Many diners along Route 66 have been serving up hearty breakfasts, burgers, and milkshakes for decades. Whether it's a greasy spoon or a retro diner, these spots are a reflection of small-town hospitality and the heart of Route 66 culture.

- **Handmade Goods and Souvenirs:** Small towns are full of locally owned shops that sell handmade goods, antiques, and one-of-a-kind treasures. These stores offer unique souvenirs that you won't find in chain stores, and they're often run by locals who are eager to share the town's history with visitors. From handcrafted pottery to vintage Route 66 memorabilia, you're sure to find something special to take home.

The People

What truly makes small-town America stand out is its people. The residents of these towns are often deeply connected to their community and proud of their history. Visitors are often struck by the warmth and hospitality of the locals, who are more than happy to share their stories, traditions, and insights into life along Route 66.

- **Friendly Conversations:** Small towns encourage interaction between locals and visitors. Whether you're in a local diner or at a roadside attraction, you'll likely find yourself in a conversation with a local who is eager to share their knowledge of the town's history, culture, and landmarks. These friendly chats are often one of the highlights of the trip, offering a deeper connection to the community.

- **Community Events:** Many small towns have weekly or monthly events that bring people together, such as farmers' markets, craft fairs, and outdoor concerts. These events are a perfect way to experience the local culture and mingle with residents, giving you an authentic taste of small-town life.

Traditional Food and Drink

Food is a key part of small-town culture, and the dishes you'll find along Route 66 are as diverse and unique as the towns themselves. Local specialties often reflect the region's history, agriculture, and cultural influences. In these towns, food is not just about sustenance—it's about tradition, family, and bringing people together.

- **Barbecue and Comfort Food:** Many small towns in the Midwest and South are famous for their barbecue, with smoky ribs, pulled pork sandwiches, and tangy sauces that have been passed down for generations. In other areas, you'll find hearty comfort foods like meatloaf, fried chicken, and mashed potatoes, often served with homemade pies for dessert.

- **Regional Dishes:** Each region along Route 66 has its own unique culinary tradition. In New Mexico, for example, you'll find dishes featuring green chiles and spicy salsas. In Oklahoma and Texas, you'll encounter classic chili and Tex-Mex dishes. And in the more northern towns, expect to see hearty stews and homemade bread, often made using family recipes.

Chapter 7: Accommodations

When it comes to Route 66, your journey isn't complete without finding the right place to rest your head. From quirky motels that capture the spirit of the road to modern hotels and scenic campsites, there's something for every type of traveler.

Best Motels
1. The Blue Swallow Motel (Tucumcari, New Mexico)

The Blue Swallow Motel

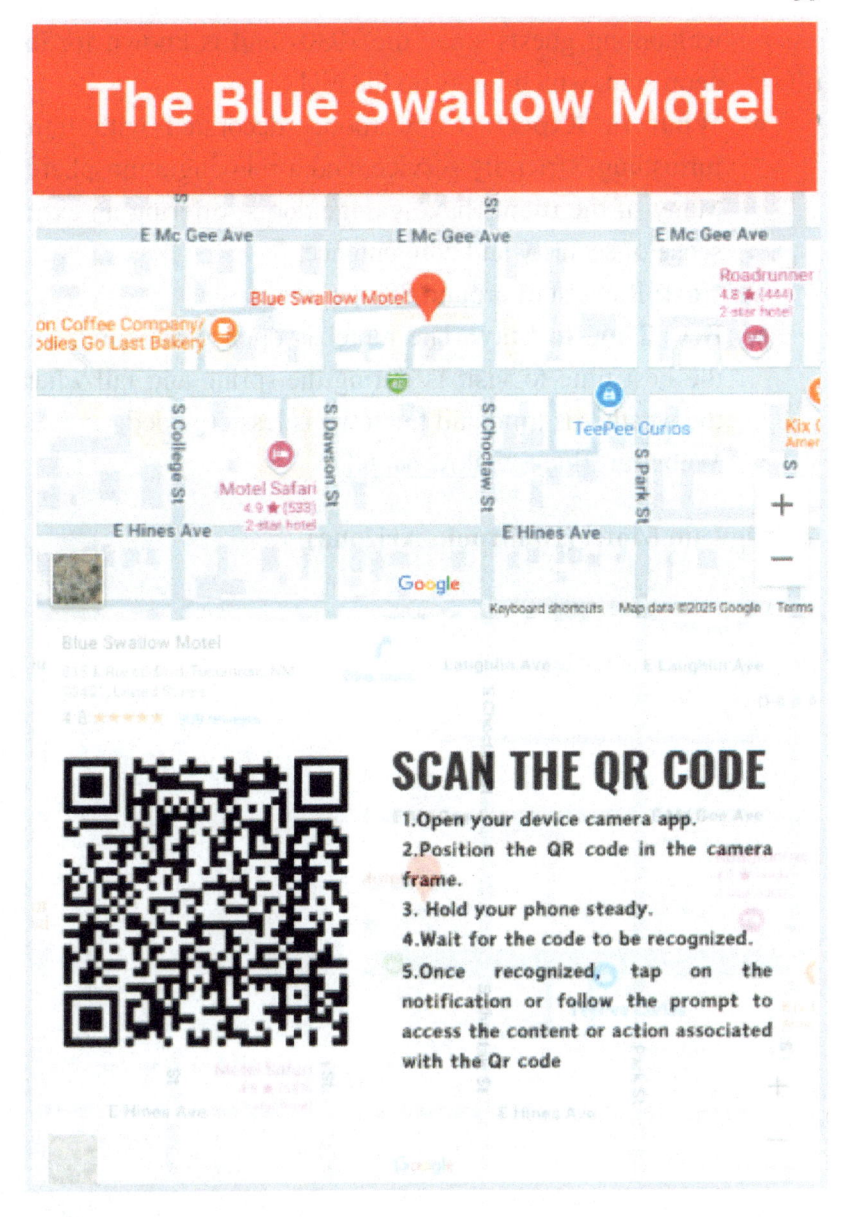

SCAN THE QR CODE
1. Open your device camera app.
2. Position the QR code in the camera frame.
3. Hold your phone steady.
4. Wait for the code to be recognized.
5. Once recognized, tap on the notification or follow the prompt to access the content or action associated with the Qr code

- **Description:** A Route 66 classic, the **Blue Swallow Motel** is an iconic stop for travelers seeking a vintage motel experience. This charming property has been

welcoming guests since the 1930s and is known for its neon sign, which lights up the night.
- **What to Expect:** Cozy rooms decorated with retro furnishings, friendly service, and a relaxing atmosphere. Many of the rooms have garage doors, offering an extra sense of security and convenience.
- **Cost:** Rates start around $80 per night.
- **Best Time to Stay:** The motel is open year-round, but the best time to visit is during the spring and fall when the weather is mild and the town is less crowded.
- **Website:** Blue Swallow Motel

2. Wigwam Motel (Holbrook, Arizona)

Wigwam Motel

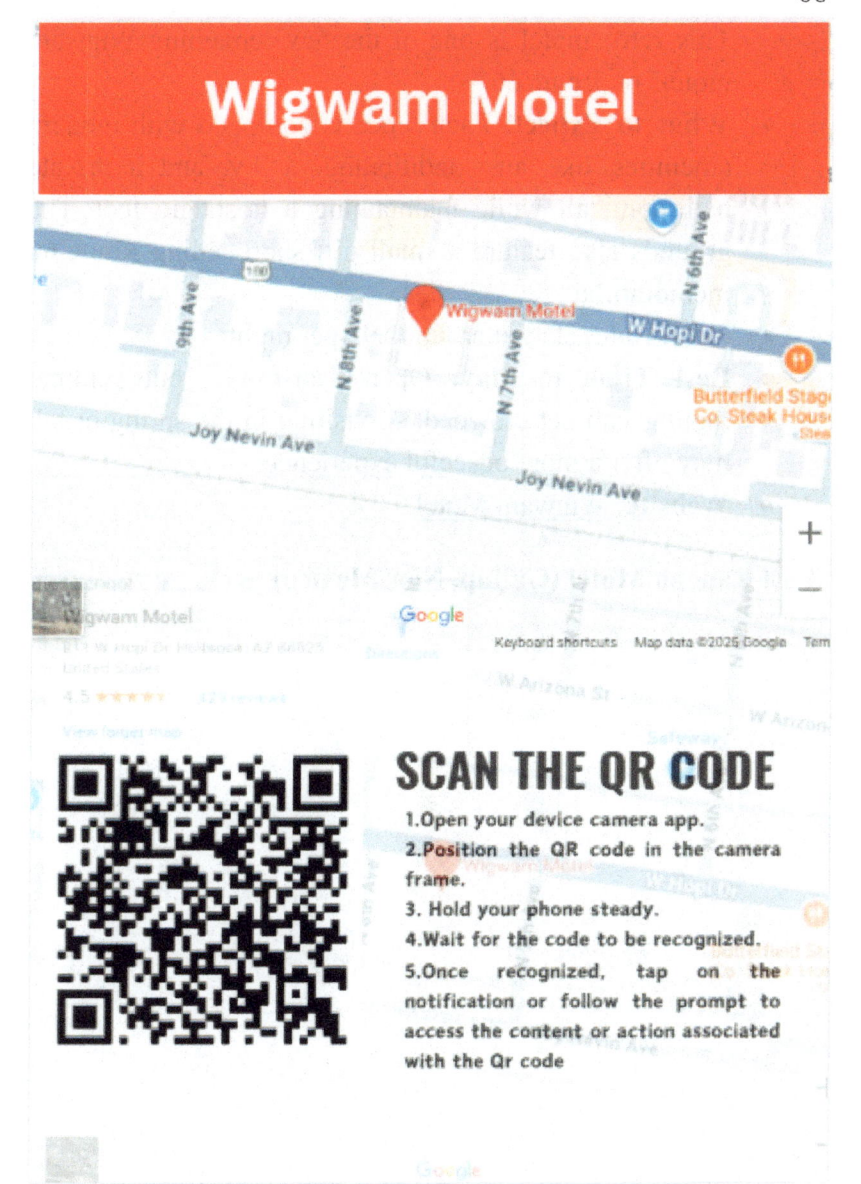

SCAN THE QR CODE
1. Open your device camera app.
2. Position the QR code in the camera frame.
3. Hold your phone steady.
4. Wait for the code to be recognized.
5. Once recognized, tap on the notification or follow the prompt to access the content or action associated with the Qr code

- **Description:** For a truly unique experience, the **Wigwam Motel** in Holbrook offers travelers the chance to sleep in one of the famous tepee-shaped buildings.

This retro motel is one of the few remaining Wigwam motels on Route 66.
- **What to Expect:** Each tepee is equipped with modern amenities like air conditioning, a TV, and a private bathroom, all while maintaining a nostalgic feel. The grounds also feature a small gift shop selling Route 66 memorabilia.
- **Cost:** Rates start at around $95 per night.
- **Best Time to Stay:** Open year-round, but summer months can get crowded, so visiting in the spring or fall may offer a more peaceful experience.
- **Website:** Wigwam Motel

3. El Rancho Motel (Gallup, New Mexico)

El Rancho Motel

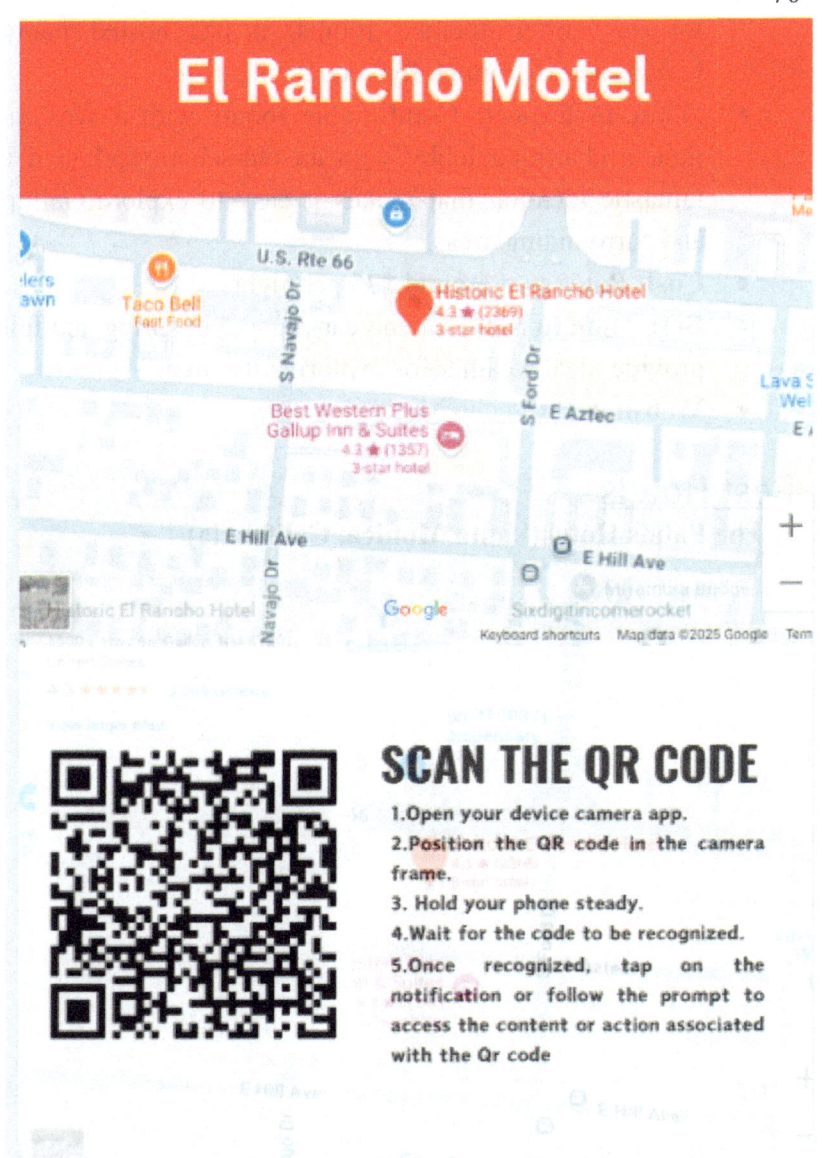

SCAN THE QR CODE
1. Open your device camera app.
2. Position the QR code in the camera frame.
3. Hold your phone steady.
4. Wait for the code to be recognized.
5. Once recognized, tap on the notification or follow the prompt to access the content or action associated with the Qr code

- **Description:** Located in Gallup, New Mexico, **El Rancho Motel** offers a throwback to the days when Route 66 was the main highway across the U.S. Known

for its Western-themed rooms, it has hosted many famous actors from Hollywood's golden age.
- **What to Expect:** Comfortable rooms with a Western flair, a charming lobby with an old-school feel, and a fantastic location that makes it easy to explore Gallup and surrounding areas.
- **Cost:** Rates start around $75 per night.
- **Best Time to Stay:** Open year-round, but spring and fall provide ideal weather for exploring the area.
- **Website:** El Rancho Motel

Best Hotels
1. The Palms Hotel (Santa Monica, California)

The Palms Hotel

SCAN THE QR CODE

1. Open your device camera app.
2. Position the QR code in the camera frame.
3. Hold your phone steady.
4. Wait for the code to be recognized.
5. Once recognized, tap on the notification or follow the prompt to access the content or action associated with the Qr code

- **Description:** Located just a short walk from the beach, **The Palms Hotel** offers a stylish, boutique experience with easy access to Santa Monica's iconic pier and

shops. This hotel blends modern amenities with a laid-back coastal atmosphere.
- **What to Expect:** Stylish rooms with sleek, contemporary design, outdoor pools, and a courtyard garden. The hotel is pet-friendly, making it a great option for travelers with pets.
- **Cost:** Rates start around $180 per night.
- **Best Time to Stay:** Santa Monica is a popular destination year-round, but spring and fall offer milder temperatures and fewer tourists.
- **Website:** [The Palms Hotel](#)

2. The Drury Inn & Suites (St. Louis, Missouri)

The Drury Inn & Suites

SCAN THE QR CODE
1. Open your device camera app.
2. Position the QR code in the camera frame.
3. Hold your phone steady.
4. Wait for the code to be recognized.
5. Once recognized, tap on the notification or follow the prompt to access the content or action associated with the Qr code

- **Description:** The **Drury Inn & Suites** in St. Louis offers a modern, convenient stay with exceptional amenities. The hotel is located near the Gateway Arch

and downtown St. Louis, making it an ideal base for exploring the city.
- **What to Expect:** Spacious rooms, a fitness center, a hot breakfast, and an evening "kickback" with free snacks and drinks. It's perfect for families and business travelers alike.
- **Cost:** Rates start around $150 per night.
- **Best Time to Stay:** The hotel is open year-round, but spring and fall offer pleasant weather for sightseeing in St. Louis.
- **Website:** [Drury Inn & Suites](#)

3. The Phoenician (Scottsdale, Arizona)

The Phoenician

SCAN THE QR CODE

1. Open your device camera app.
2. Position the QR code in the camera frame.
3. Hold your phone steady.
4. Wait for the code to be recognized.
5. Once recognized, tap on the notification or follow the prompt to access the content or action associated with the Qr code

- **Description:** For travelers looking for a luxurious hotel experience, **The Phoenician** in Scottsdale is a stunning

77

resort that offers unparalleled service, beautiful desert views, and a wealth of amenities.
- **What to Expect:** Spacious rooms and suites, an expansive spa, world-class dining, and an outdoor pool. The resort is perfect for those looking to indulge in a high-end experience during their Route 66 journey.
- **Cost:** Rates start around $350 per night.
- **Best Time to Stay:** Spring and fall are ideal for visiting Scottsdale, as temperatures are more moderate compared to the extreme heat of summer.
- **Website:** [The Phoenician](#)

4. The Drury Plaza Hotel (Oklahoma City, Oklahoma)

The Drury Plaza Hotel

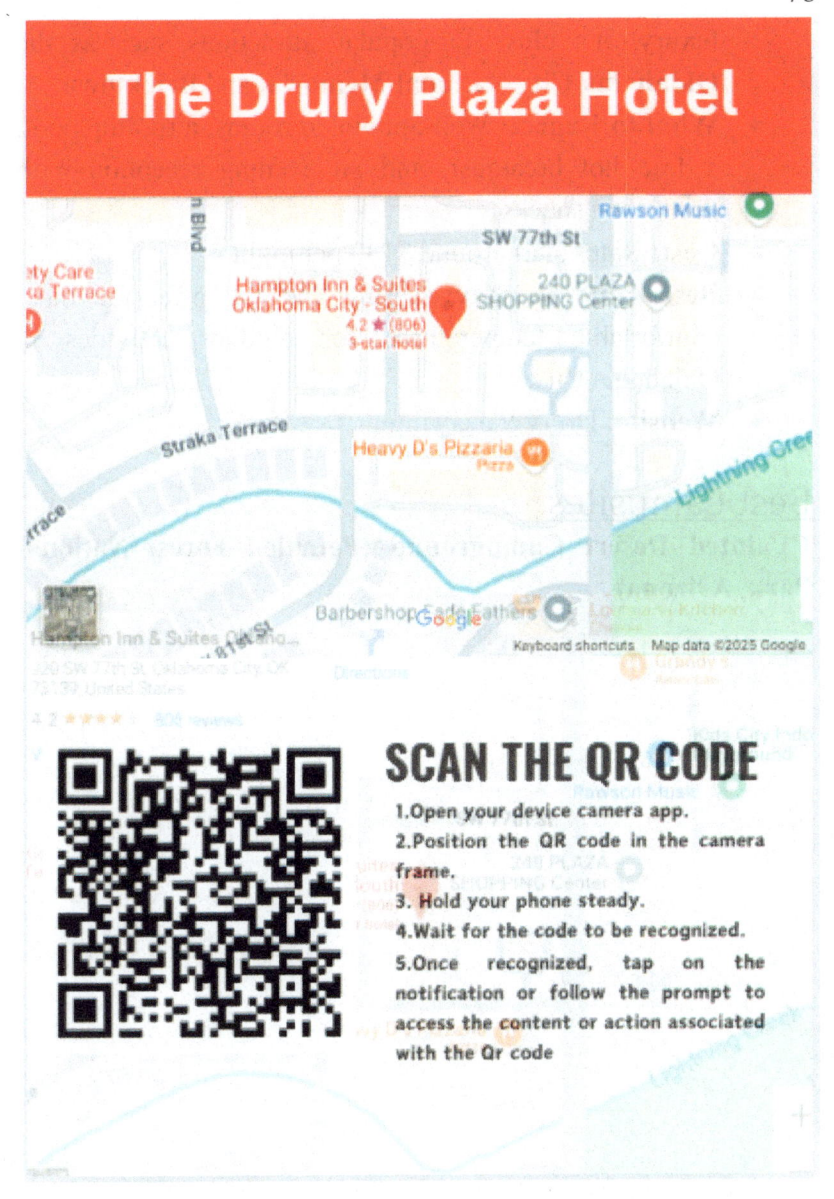

SCAN THE QR CODE

1. Open your device camera app.
2. Position the QR code in the camera frame.
3. Hold your phone steady.
4. Wait for the code to be recognized.
5. Once recognized, tap on the notification or follow the prompt to access the content or action associated with the Qr code

- **Description:** Located in downtown Oklahoma City, the **Drury Plaza Hotel** is a fantastic choice for those looking for comfort and convenience with a touch of

luxury. It's close to popular attractions such as the **Oklahoma City National Memorial** and **Bricktown**.
- **What to Expect:** Well-appointed rooms, a rooftop pool, a free hot breakfast, and an evening reception with drinks and snacks.
- **Cost:** Rates start around $130 per night.
- **Best Time to Stay:** Spring and fall offer the most comfortable temperatures for outdoor activities in Oklahoma City.
- **Website:** Drury Plaza Hotel

Best Campsites
1.Painted Desert Campground (Petrified Forest National Park, Arizona)

Painted Desert Campground

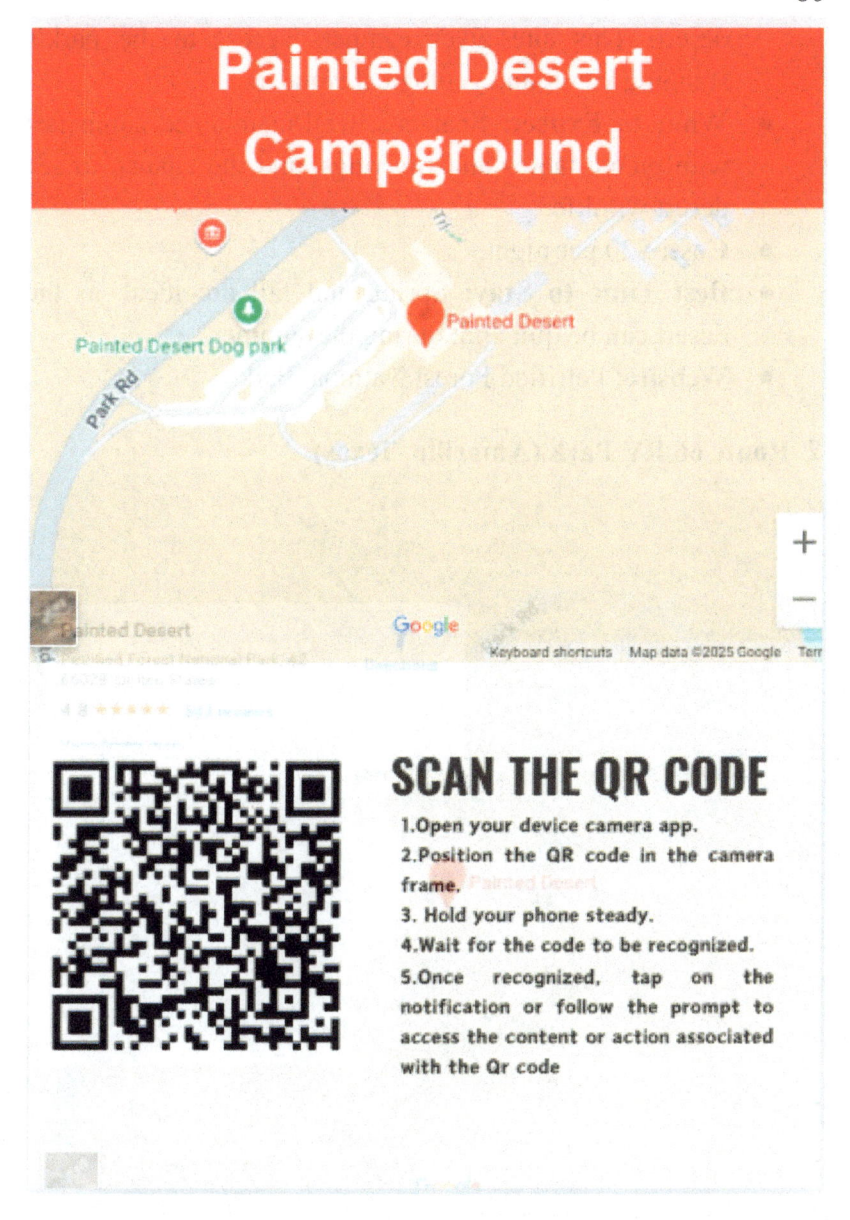

SCAN THE QR CODE
1. Open your device camera app.
2. Position the QR code in the camera frame.
3. Hold your phone steady.
4. Wait for the code to be recognized.
5. Once recognized, tap on the notification or follow the prompt to access the content or action associated with the Qr code

- **Description:** Located within **Petrified Forest National Park**, the **Painted Desert Campground** offers a peaceful and scenic spot to camp in the heart of the

desert. This site gives campers access to the park's stunning views and geological wonders.
- **What to Expect:** Spacious, well-maintained campsites with picnic tables and fire rings, and the chance to see desert wildlife.
- **Cost:** $20 per night.
- **Best Time to Stay:** Spring and fall are ideal, as the desert can be quite hot during the summer.
- **Website:** Petrified Forest National Park

2. Route 66 RV Park (Amarillo, Texas)

Route 66 RV Park

SCAN THE QR CODE
1. Open your device camera app.
2. Position the QR code in the camera frame.
3. Hold your phone steady.
4. Wait for the code to be recognized.
5. Once recognized, tap on the notification or follow the prompt to access the content or action associated with the Qr code

- **Description:** If you're traveling by RV, the **Route 66 RV Park** in Amarillo offers a convenient and comfortable spot to park for the night. The park is located near many

local attractions, including the Cadillac Ranch and the Route 66 Historic District.
- **What to Expect:** Full hook-ups for RVs, clean restrooms, and easy access to Route 66 attractions. The park is also pet-friendly, making it a great choice for families traveling with pets.
- **Cost:** $35 per night for RV spaces.
- **Best Time to Stay:** Open year-round, but spring and fall offer the best weather for RV camping.
- **Website:** Route 66 RV Park

3. KOA Campground (Flagstaff, Arizona)

KOA Campground

SCAN THE QR CODE
1. Open your device camera app.
2. Position the QR code in the camera frame.
3. Hold your phone steady.
4. Wait for the code to be recognized.
5. Once recognized, tap on the notification or follow the prompt to access the content or action associated with the Qr code

- **Description:** Located just outside Flagstaff, the **KOA Campground** offers a well-equipped, family-friendly camping experience in the beautiful Arizona wilderness.

The campground features amenities like a heated pool, bike rentals, and a pet park.
- **What to Expect:** Tent sites, RV spaces, and cabin rentals. The campground is set against a stunning backdrop of trees and mountains, perfect for outdoor enthusiasts.
- **Cost:** Tent sites start at $25 per night; RV spaces start at $50 per night.
- **Best Time to Stay:** Summer for outdoor activities, or spring and fall for milder temperatures.
- **Website:** KOA Campground Flagstaff

4.Santa Monica State Beach Campground (Santa Monica, California)

Santa Monica State Beach Campground

SCAN THE QR CODE

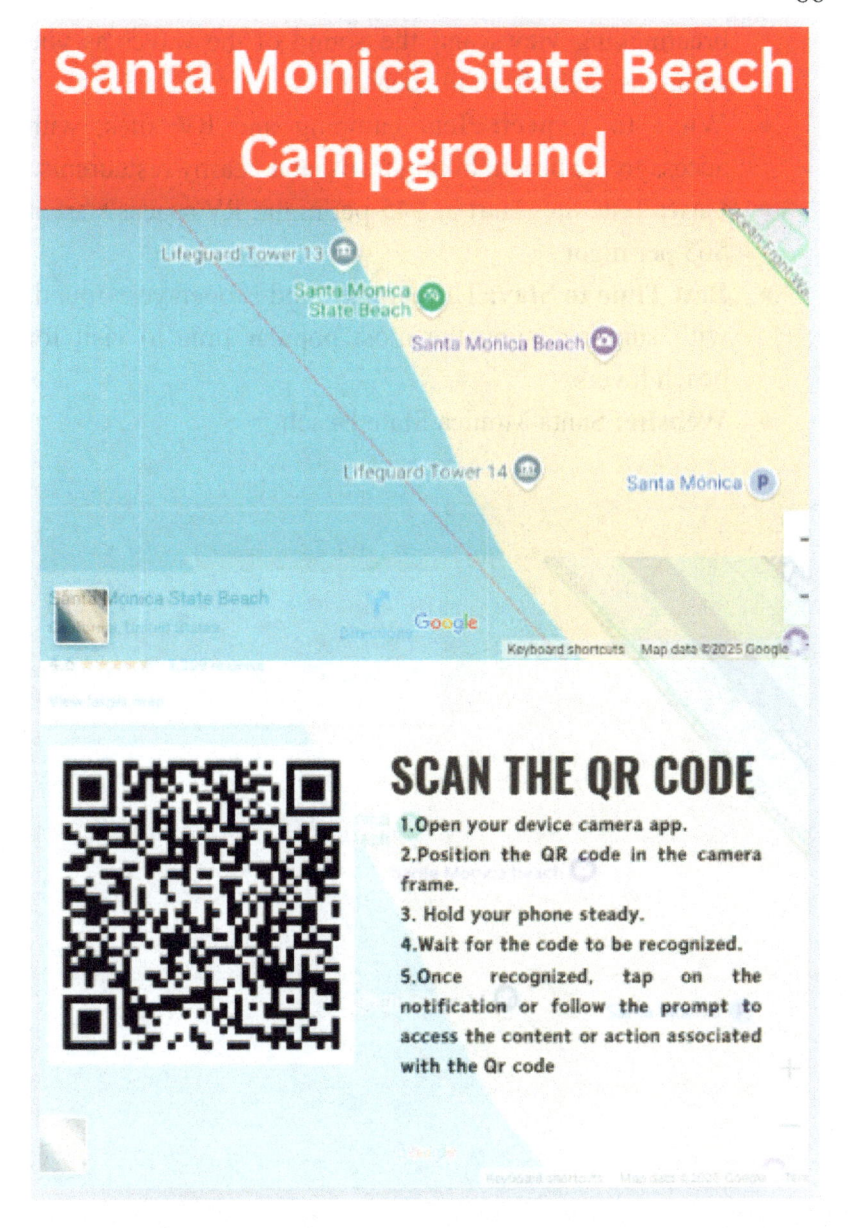

1. Open your device camera app.
2. Position the QR code in the camera frame.
3. Hold your phone steady.
4. Wait for the code to be recognized.
5. Once recognized, tap on the notification or follow the prompt to access the content or action associated with the Qr code

- **Description:** If you're looking to camp near the beach, **Santa Monica State Beach Campground** offers an incredible spot right by the Pacific Ocean. Enjoy

breathtaking views and the sound of the waves as you camp just steps from the beach.
- **What to Expect:** Tent camping and RV sites, with access to the beach, hiking trails, and nearby restaurants.
- **Cost:** Tent sites start at $45 per night; RV spaces start at $65 per night.
- **Best Time to Stay:** The campground is open year-round, with summer being the most popular time to visit for beach lovers.
- **Website:** Santa Monica State Beach

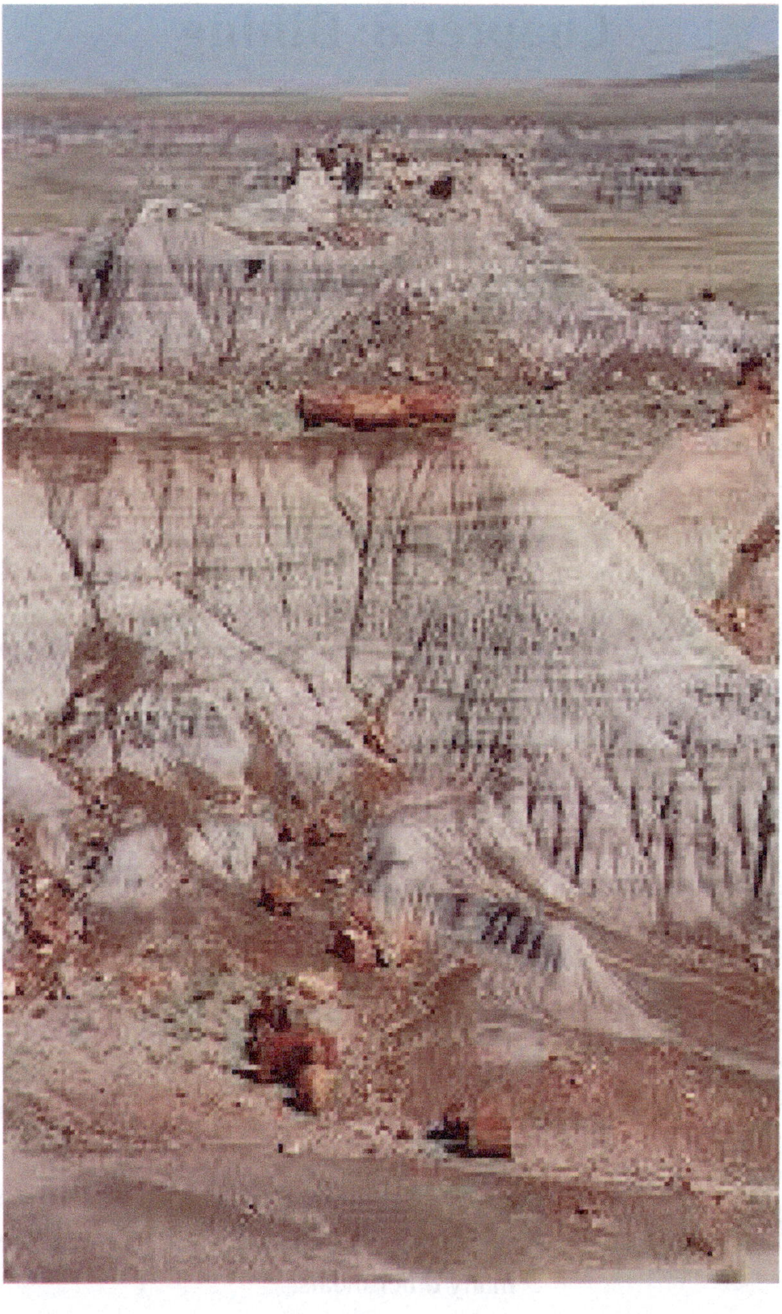

Chapter 8: Dining

Classic American Diners and Must-Try Meals

1. Route 66 Diners

- **What to Expect:** These iconic diners capture the spirit of the road, often offering retro décor and classic American fare.
- **Must-Try Meals:**
    - **Burgers:** From juicy beef burgers to veggie options, Route 66 diners are known for their hearty, delicious burgers.
    - **Milkshakes:** Indulge in a creamy milkshake, a timeless treat that pairs perfectly with a burger.
    - **All-Day Breakfast:** Classic diner breakfasts like pancakes, eggs, bacon, and hash browns.
    - **Fries & Sides:** Crispy fries and onion rings are essential accompaniments to many diner meals.

2. Top Classic Diner Stops

The Big Texan Steak Ranch (Amarillo, TX)
- **Address:** 7701 I-40, Amarillo, TX 79118
- **Description:** The Big Texan Steak Ranch is a true Route 66 institution, especially famous for its 72-ounce steak challenge. This classic steakhouse has been serving hearty meals to travelers since 1960.
- **Must-Try Meals:** Don't miss their legendary 72-ounce steak challenge. If you finish it, the meal is free! Otherwise, enjoy their juicy steaks, ribs, and signature sides.
- **Cost:** Meal prices vary; the 72-ounce steak challenge is free if you finish it within one hour.
- **Best Time to Visit:** It's open year-round, but it gets busy during weekends and holidays, so plan accordingly.

The Route 66 Diner (Albuquerque, NM)
- **Address:** 5210 Isleta Blvd SW, Albuquerque, NM 87105
- **Description:** The Route 66 Diner is a retro spot that offers all the classic diner dishes with a New Mexico twist. It's a perfect place to stop for a hearty meal while embracing the nostalgic vibe of Route 66.
- **Must-Try Meals:** The Green Chile Cheeseburger is a local favorite, along with classic diner breakfast options like pancakes and omelets.
- **Cost:** Burgers and meals start around $10 to $15.
- **Best Time to Visit:** It's open daily, but visiting in the morning for breakfast or in the afternoon for a relaxed lunch is ideal.

Lou Mitchell's (Chicago, IL)

- **Address:** 565 W Jackson Blvd, Chicago, IL 60661
- **Description:** Lou Mitchell's has been a Chicago landmark since 1923, and it's known for its classic diner experience and fantastic breakfast. Whether you're just starting your Route 66 journey or passing through, Lou Mitchell's is a must-stop.
- **Must-Try Meals:** Their famous omelets, fluffy pancakes, and classic hash browns. Don't miss their delicious coffee and homemade donuts.
- **Cost:** Meals range from $7 for a basic breakfast to $15 for more elaborate dishes.
- **Best Time to Visit:** It's open daily, and breakfast is served all day, so it's perfect for early risers or a relaxed start to your day.

The Big Chill (Flagstaff, AZ)

- **Address:** 45 S San Francisco St, Flagstaff, AZ 86001
- **Description:** This retro-style diner with a laid-back atmosphere offers a selection of burgers, fries, and sandwiches. It's a great place for a quick and satisfying meal after exploring the charming downtown area of Flagstaff.
- **Must-Try Meals:** The **Green Chile Cheeseburger** and **Big Chill Fries** are fan favorites, and the milkshakes are perfect for dessert.
- **Cost:** Meals start around $10.
- **Best Time to Visit:** Stop by for lunch or dinner, as it can get busy in the morning with tourists and locals alike.

Vegetarian and Vegan Options

Vegetarian and Vegan-Friendly Diner Meals

- **What to Expect:** While many Route 66 diners focus on traditional comfort food, more and more are offering vegetarian and vegan alternatives, including plant-based burgers, salads, and non-dairy shakes.
- **Must-Try Meals:**
  - **Veggie Burgers:** A staple in many diners, these come in various styles made from beans, vegetables, or soy-based patties.
  - **Vegan Tacos:** Many stops along Route 66 now serve flavorful plant-based tacos with toppings like guacamole, roasted vegetables, and black beans.
  - **Salads & Bowls:** Fresh salads with unique ingredients such as quinoa, avocado, and roasted veggies.
  - **Vegan Desserts:** Some diners and bakeries offer vegan pie, cakes, and cookies that don't compromise on taste.

2. Best Stops for Vegetarian and Vegan Options

Green New American Vegetarian (Tempe, AZ)
- **Address:** 2240 N Scottsdale Rd, Tempe, AZ 85281
- **Description:** A fully vegan restaurant that's a favorite along Route 66 for plant-based comfort food. Green serves creative and tasty dishes using fresh, organic ingredients.
- **Must-Try Meals:** The **Buffalo Cauliflower Bites**, **BBQ Tempeh Tacos**, and the famous **Vegan Cheeseburger** are excellent choices.
- **Cost:** Entrees range from $8 to $15.

- **Best Time to Visit:** It's a popular spot for lunch and dinner, but arriving earlier will ensure you avoid long wait times.

The Beet Box (Flagstaff, AZ)

- **Address:** 14 E Route 66, Flagstaff, AZ 86001
- **Description:** A cozy cafe offering a menu full of fresh and healthy vegetarian and vegan options. The Beet Box is known for its smoothies, bowls, and sandwiches that cater to plant-based diets.
- **Must-Try Meals:** Try the **Veggie Wrap**, **Vegan Buddha Bowl**, or a fresh **Acai Bowl** for a refreshing and nutritious meal.
- **Cost:** Meals range from $7 to $12.
- **Best Time to Visit:** The cafe is a great breakfast or lunch spot, especially for a quick, healthy meal before hitting the road.

Mother Road Brewing Company (Flagstaff, AZ)

- **Address:** 7 S Mikes Pike, Flagstaff, AZ 86001
- **Description:** Mother Road Brewing Company is a fantastic brewery with a laid-back atmosphere and a selection of vegan and vegetarian-friendly dishes. Perfect for a drink and a hearty meal while soaking in the local vibe.
- **Must-Try Meals:** The **Vegan Black Bean Burger**, **Vegetarian Tacos**, and the **House-made Veggie Pizza** are great choices.
- **Cost:** Meals start at around $8 to $15.

- **Best Time to Visit:** Open year-round, but it's especially nice to visit in the evening when they host local music and events.

Sweetie Pies (St. Louis, MO)

- **Address:** 225 N Euclid Ave, St. Louis, MO 63108
- **Description:** A casual dining spot offering a variety of vegan and vegetarian comfort food, from hearty entrees to fresh salads and sandwiches. Sweetie Pies is a great place for a plant-based twist on American classics.
- **Must-Try Meals:** Try the **Vegan Southern Fried Seitan**, **Grilled Veggie Tacos**, or the **Vegan Mac & Cheese**.
- **Cost:** Meals range from $10 to $20.
- **Best Time to Visit:** It's a popular spot for brunch or lunch, so visiting early in the day is ideal.

Unique Dining Experiences Along the Route

1.Historic and Iconic Eateries

- **What to Expect:** Route 66 is home to a number of historic and iconic eateries that add a unique twist to your dining experience. From themed restaurants to roadside stands, these spots are filled with character and often serve up classic American dishes with a local touch.
- **Must-Try Experiences:**
    - **Themed Restaurants:** Many spots along Route 66 have embraced the nostalgia of the road with fun and quirky themes,

offering a unique atmosphere that takes you back in time.
- **Roadside Stands:** Local food trucks or roadside stands often serve regional specialties, from tacos in New Mexico to BBQ in Texas.
- **Drive-ins and Drive-throughs:** Old-school drive-ins still allow you to enjoy a meal without leaving your car, bringing back memories of the 1950s diner culture.

2.Best Unique Dining Experiences

1. The Blue Hole (Santa Rosa, NM)

- **Address:** 7 Blue Hole Rd, Santa Rosa, NM 88435
- **Description:** A unique roadside diner located next to a stunning natural spring pool, offering the chance to enjoy a meal and take a dip.
- **Must-Try Meals:** Try the **Fried Chicken**, **Burgers**, or a light salad for a refreshing meal after swimming in the clear, cool waters of the Blue Hole.
- **Cost:** Meals range from $8 to $15.
- **Best Time to Visit:** Open year-round, but spring and summer are especially popular when the swimming area is open.

2. Café 66 (Seligman, AZ)

- **Address:** 22535 W Route 66, Seligman, AZ 86337
- **Description:** Located in a town that's a real Route 66 gem, **Café 66** serves up traditional diner food with a

nostalgic vibe. The café is a great place for a casual, memorable meal.
- **Must-Try Meals:** Their classic **Burgers, Milkshakes**, and **Country Fried Steak** are crowd favorites.
- **Cost:** Meals range from $8 to $15.
- **Best Time to Visit:** Stop in for a mid-day break while exploring Seligman, especially on a road trip.

3.. **The Galley Restaurant (Santa Monica, CA)**

- **Address:** 1235 7th St, Santa Monica, CA 90401
- **Description:** Located near the beach, **The Galley Restaurant** offers seafood and American classics in a relaxed and casual setting, just minutes from the Santa Monica Pier.
- **Must-Try Meals:** Enjoy their famous **Lobster Roll, Fish Tacos,** and **Grilled Salmon**.
- **Cost:** Meals range from $15 to $25.
- **Best Time to Visit:** Stop in for a meal after a beach day, or enjoy a relaxed dinner with ocean views in the evening.

Chapter 9: Route 66 Road Trip Activities

Hiking and Outdoor Adventures

Route 66 runs through diverse landscapes, from deserts to mountains, forests to plains. For outdoor enthusiasts, this iconic highway offers countless opportunities for hiking and exploring the great outdoors. Whether you're looking for a short scenic walk or a challenging backcountry hike, you'll find it along the route.

1. **Petrified Forest National Park (Arizona)**
    - **What to Do:** Explore the park's striking **petrified wood forests** and colorful desert vistas. The **Blue Mesa Trail** is a must-see for its unique geological formations.
    - **Best Hike:** The **Painted Desert Rim Trail** offers a relatively easy hike with stunning views of the desert and its colorful, layered rock formations.
    - **Distance:** Varies from 1 to 3 miles, depending on the trail.
    - **Difficulty:** Easy to moderate.

2. **Saguaro National Park (Arizona)**
    - **What to Do:** Hike through the iconic **Saguaro Cactus** forest and explore the Sonoran Desert. This park is home to towering saguaro cacti, some of the oldest and largest in the world.
    - **Best Hike:** The **Signal Hill Trail** offers a short hike with a chance to see ancient petroglyphs and panoramic desert views.
    - **Distance:** 1.2 miles (round trip).
    - **Difficulty:** Moderate.
3. **Grand Canyon National Park (Arizona)**
    - **What to Do:** A visit to Route 66 wouldn't be complete without exploring the **Grand Canyon**. There are a variety of trails, from rim walks to challenging hikes down to the Colorado River.
    - **Best Hike:** The **Bright Angel Trail** offers an easy-to-moderate descent into the canyon with stunning views.
    - **Distance:** Varies, but a popular day hike is about 4.5 miles to **Indian Garden**.
    - **Difficulty:** Moderate to difficult.
4. **Cahokia Mounds State Historic Site (Illinois)**
    - **What to Do:** Visit the ancient **Cahokia Mounds**, a UNESCO World Heritage site, and hike the trails that wind through this fascinating archaeological park.
    - **Best Hike:** The **Monks Mound Trail** offers a view of the largest prehistoric earthwork in North America.
    - **Distance:** 1 mile (easy).
    - **Difficulty:** Easy.

Local Shopping and Souvenir Spots

One of the joys of a Route 66 road trip is the opportunity to collect souvenirs and mementos that reflect the unique charm of the highway. Whether you're looking for kitschy roadside trinkets, handmade crafts, or vintage Route 66 memorabilia, you'll find plenty of shops to explore along the route.

1. **The Route 66 Gift Shop (Chicago, Illinois)**
    - **What to Expect:** This shop is the perfect place to pick up official Route 66 souvenirs, from t-shirts and mugs to postcards and vintage signs.
    - **Specialty Items:** Route 66-themed memorabilia, local artisan crafts, and vintage highway relics.
2. **The Blue Swallow Motel Gift Shop (Tucumcari, New Mexico)**
    - **What to Expect:** Along with being a nostalgic place to stay, the **Blue Swallow Motel** offers unique gifts and memorabilia that celebrate the motel's long history along Route 66.

- **Specialty Items:** Vintage Route 66 postcards, shirts, and local souvenirs that highlight the area's retro vibe.
3. **The Mother Road Market (Tulsa, Oklahoma)**
    - **What to Expect:** A modern market celebrating Route 66 culture with local vendors offering handmade goods, vintage items, and delicious local food.
    - **Specialty Items:** Locally made jewelry, art, food products, and classic Route 66 apparel.
4. **Santa Monica Pier Shops (Santa Monica, California)**
    - **What to Expect:** At the end of Route 66, the shops at **Santa Monica Pier** offer a variety of souvenirs to mark the end of your journey.
    - **Specialty Items:** Beachwear, California-themed gifts, and classic Route 66 memorabilia, including surfboard-inspired items.

Photography Tips for Route 66

Route 66 is a photographer's dream, offering a wide array of landscapes, historic sites, and quirky roadside attractions. Whether you're using a professional camera or your smartphone, there are several key tips to help you capture the essence of your Route 66 adventure.

1. **Golden Hour Photos**
    - **Tip:** The best time for capturing stunning photos is during the golden hour—just after sunrise and before sunset. The soft, warm light will enhance the colors of the landscapes and provide beautiful shadows.

- **Where to Go:** The **Painted Desert** in Arizona and **Cahokia Mounds** in Illinois are perfect spots for golden hour photography.
2. **Capture the Neon Signs**
    - **Tip:** Many towns along Route 66 are famous for their vintage neon signs. To capture the best shots, photograph them at night when they light up in all their glory.
    - **Where to Go:** The **Blue Swallow Motel** in Tucumcari, New Mexico, and **The Route 66 Diner** in Albuquerque, New Mexico, are excellent spots to photograph neon signs.
3. **Use Leading Lines**
    - **Tip:** Use the natural lines of the road to lead the viewer's eye through the photo. Roads, fences, and bridges make excellent leading lines in your Route 66 shots.
    - **Where to Go:** The **long, straight roads** of Route 66 in New Mexico or Arizona are perfect for this technique.

Family-Friendly Activities

Route 66 offers plenty of family-friendly activities that are perfect for making memories with loved ones. Whether you have little ones, teenagers, or a mix of both, these activities will entertain everyone.

1. **The Route 66 Visitor Center (Tulsa, Oklahoma)**
    - **What to Do:** Stop by this interactive center to learn about the history of Route 66 through fun exhibits, educational displays, and historical artifacts.

- Best For: Children and teens interested in history and education.
2. **Santa Monica Pier (Santa Monica, California)**
   - **What to Do:** With an amusement park, aquarium, arcade, and family-friendly restaurants, the **Santa Monica Pier** is the perfect spot to spend a day of fun for the entire family.
   - **Best For:** Families with young children who will love the rides and ocean views.
3. **The Oklahoma Route 66 Museum (Clinton, Oklahoma)**
   - **What to Do:** This museum offers an interactive and educational experience with displays on the history of the highway, old cars, and Route 66 memorabilia.
   - **Best For:** Families with young children and history buffs.
4. **Arizona-Sonora Desert Museum (Tucson, Arizona)**
   - **What to Do:** Explore the diverse flora and fauna of the desert at this outdoor museum, which features wildlife, botanical gardens, and interactive exhibits.
   - **Best For:** Families with children who love animals and nature.

Chapter 10: Itinerary Options

Route 66 is a legendary road trip, and depending on how much time you have, you can tailor your adventure to suit your schedule. Whether you're looking for a 10-day adventure, a more leisurely 2-3 week road trip, or even a quick weekend getaway, there's a Route 66 itinerary that's perfect for you. Let's look at three practical options that ensure you get the most out of your time on the Mother Road without feeling rushed.

10-Day Adventure

If you're pressed for time but still want to hit the highlights, a 10-day Route 66 trip is a great way to experience the magic of the highway while leaving time for rest and exploration. This itinerary focuses on key attractions, while also allowing enough time for relaxation.

Day 1: Chicago, Illinois to Springfield, Illinois

- **Distance:** 200 miles (3-4 hours)
- **What to Do:** Start your adventure in **Chicago**, where you can explore a few iconic spots like **Willis Tower** or

the **Route 66 Museum**. Afterward, head to **Springfield**, home of **Abraham Lincoln's Presidential Library** and **Route 66-related landmarks**.
- **Highlights:** Willis Tower, Route 66 Museum, Abraham Lincoln Presidential Library.
- **Stay:** Springfield has charming local motels and small boutique hotels.

Day 2: Springfield, Illinois to St. Louis, Missouri

- **Distance:** 100 miles (1.5-2 hours)
- **What to Do:** Continue your Route 66 journey to **St. Louis**. Take in the **Gateway Arch** and visit the **Route 66 Historical District**. You'll also have time to stroll through the city's iconic neighborhoods.
- **Highlights:** Gateway Arch, Route 66 Historic District, local dining spots.
- **Stay:** Choose from budget hotels near the Arch or quaint downtown motels.

Day 3: St. Louis, Missouri to Springfield, Missouri

- **Distance:** 200 miles (3-4 hours)
- **What to Do:** On your way to **Springfield**, stop at a few Route 66 landmarks such as **The Chain of Rocks Bridge**. In Springfield, visit **Route 66 Car Museum** and the **Historic Downtown**.
- **Highlights:** The Chain of Rocks Bridge, Route 66 Car Museum.
- **Stay:** Springfield has both cozy motels and well-known hotel chains.

Day 4: Springfield, Missouri to Tulsa, Oklahoma

- **Distance:** 180 miles (3 hours)
- **What to Do:** Arrive in **Tulsa**, known for its rich Art Deco architecture. Spend time visiting the **Philbrook Museum of Art** or walking through **Tulsa's Route 66 Historic District**.
- **Highlights:** Philbrook Museum of Art, Tulsa's Art Deco District.
- **Stay:** Plenty of local motels, or more modern hotels in the downtown area.

Day 5: Tulsa, Oklahoma to Amarillo, Texas

- **Distance:** 260 miles (4 hours)
- **What to Do:** Head to **Amarillo**, known for the famous **Cadillac Ranch** and **Big Texan Steak Ranch**. Take in the local history and the quirky roadside attractions.
- **Highlights:** Cadillac Ranch, Big Texan Steak Ranch.
- **Stay:** Amarillo has a variety of motels and charming inns.

Day 6: Amarillo, Texas to Albuquerque, New Mexico

- **Distance:** 290 miles (4.5 hours)
- **What to Do:** Cross into New Mexico and explore **Tucumcari's** Route 66 murals and motels. Then head to **Albuquerque**, where you can explore **Old Town Albuquerque** and stop by the **Route 66 Historical Museum**.
- **Highlights:** Tucumcari murals, Old Town Albuquerque, Route 66 Museum.
- **Stay:** Albuquerque has plenty of motels and mid-range hotels with easy access to the historic district.

Day 7: Albuquerque, New Mexico to Flagstaff, Arizona

- **Distance:** 330 miles (5 hours)
- **What to Do:** Visit the **Petrified Forest National Park** and **Painted Desert**, then continue to **Flagstaff**, where you can explore the **Route 66 Historic District** and enjoy local art and food.
- **Highlights:** Petrified Forest, Painted Desert, Flagstaff Historic District.
- **Stay:** Flagstaff offers a variety of historic motels and well-known hotel chains.

Day 8: Flagstaff, Arizona to Grand Canyon National Park

- **Distance:** 80 miles (1.5 hours)
- **What to Do:** Take a day trip to the **Grand Canyon**. Spend time walking along the **South Rim** or hike a section of the **Bright Angel Trail** for breathtaking views.
- **Highlights:** Grand Canyon, Bright Angel Trail.
- **Stay:** Stay in **Grand Canyon Village** or head back to Flagstaff.

Day 9: Grand Canyon to Seligman, Arizona

- **Distance:** 120 miles (2 hours)
- **What to Do:** Explore **Seligman**, a small town rich in Route 66 history. Visit the **Route 66 Gift Shop** and take photos of the nostalgic landmarks.
- **Highlights:** Route 66 Gift Shops, Seligman's vintage charm.
- **Stay:** Budget motels and unique roadside motels in Seligman.

Day 10: Seligman, Arizona to Santa Monica, California

- **Distance:** 350 miles (6 hours)
- **What to Do:** Complete your Route 66 journey by heading to **Santa Monica**, where you can enjoy the **Santa Monica Pier**, relax on the beach, and take in the ocean breeze.
- **Highlights:** Santa Monica Pier, beach views.
- **Stay:** Santa Monica offers both luxury hotels and budget motels.

Extended 2-3 Week Road Trip

If you have more time to explore and want to truly savor the Route 66 experience, consider a **2-3 week road trip**. This extended itinerary allows you to explore each state in more depth and discover additional landmarks, scenic byways, and hidden gems along the route.

Week 1: Chicago to Oklahoma City

- **What to Do:** Spend 3-4 days in Chicago to visit its iconic landmarks like **Willis Tower** and **The Art Institute**. Then head west to **St. Louis** and take your time exploring the **Gateway Arch**, before continuing to **Tulsa**, **Amarillo**, and **Albuquerque**.
- **Additional Stops: Route 66 Museum** in Pontiac, **The Blue Swallow Motel** in Tucumcari, and **Cadillac Ranch** in Amarillo.
- **Stay:** Stay in local motels, boutique hotels, and historic inns along the way.

Week 2: Oklahoma City to Arizona

- **What to Do:** Continue through **Oklahoma City** to **Flagstaff**, and explore more of **Petrified Forest National Park**. Add a day trip to the **Grand Canyon** and visit nearby **Sedona** for its stunning red rock formations.
- **Additional Stops: Mother Road Museum** in Barstow and **Route 66 Village** in Tulsa.
- **Stay:** Plenty of motels and campgrounds in national parks and cities.

Week 3: Arizona to California

- **What to Do:** Explore more of Arizona's unique desert landscapes, and take your time driving through **California**. Spend a day in **Santa Monica**, where Route 66 officially ends. Don't forget to enjoy the beach, pier, and local shops before wrapping up your journey.
- **Additional Stops: Santa Monica Pier**, **Venice Beach**, and **Malibu**.
- **Stay:** Hotel options in **Santa Monica** range from budget motels to upscale hotels by the beach.

Weekend Getaway

If you only have a weekend, you can still experience a bit of Route 66. A short **weekend getaway** option focuses on the heart of the route, starting in **Chicago** and ending in **St. Louis**.

Day 1: Chicago, Illinois

- **What to Do:** Spend your first day exploring **Chicago**, the starting point of Route 66. Visit the **Willis Tower, The Art Institute**, and enjoy a deep-dish pizza.

- **Highlights:** Willis Tower, Millennium Park, Art Institute of Chicago.

Day 2: Chicago to St. Louis, Missouri

- **Distance:** 300 miles (4-5 hours)
- **What to Do:** Head south to **St. Louis**. Visit the **Gateway Arch** and walk through the **Route 66 Historical District**. Enjoy a classic St. Louis-style **BBQ** and explore the city's vibrant downtown.
- **Highlights:** Gateway Arch, Route 66 District, St. Louis BBQ.

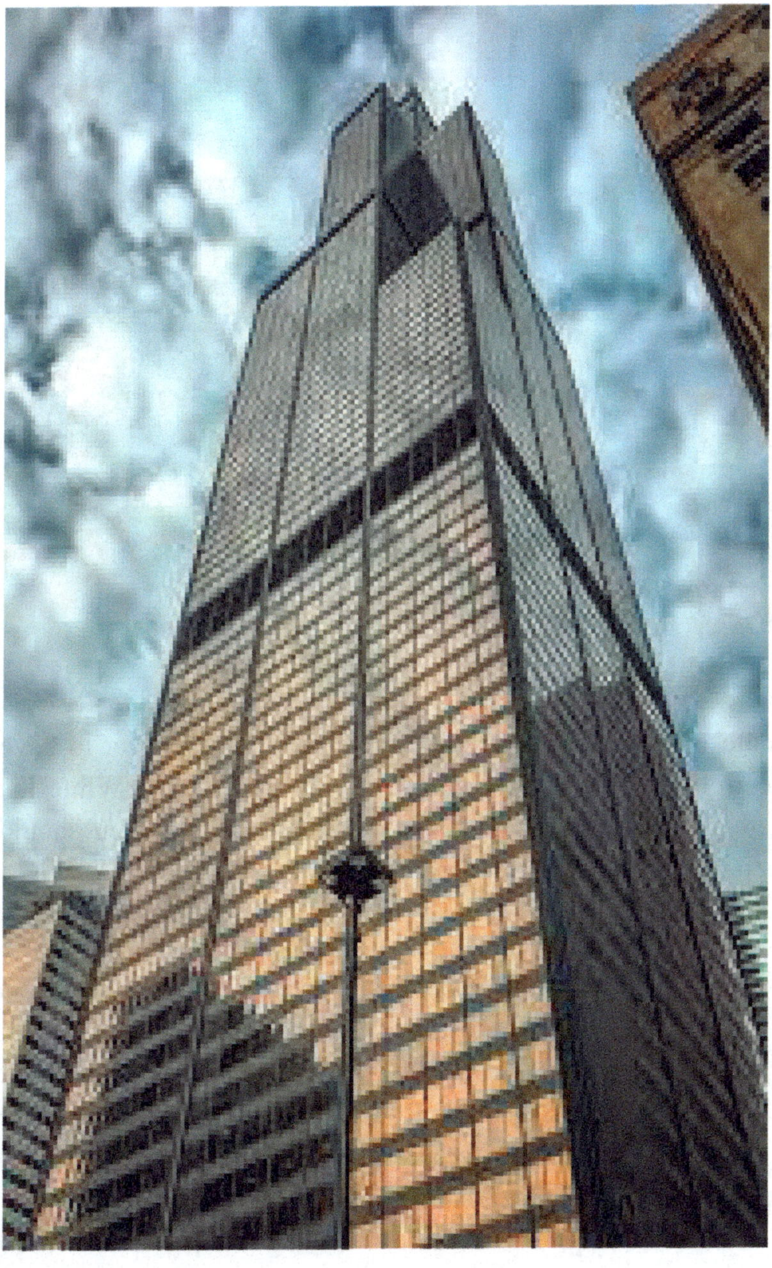

Chapter 11: Practical Travel Tips

Navigating the Route

Route 66 stretches over 2,400 miles, so it's important to have the right tools to navigate this legendary highway. While the road itself is well-marked, there are a few things you should keep in mind for a smooth trip.

1. **Maps and Apps**
    - **What to Use:** Old-school paper maps can be a fun and nostalgic way to navigate, but digital tools like **Google Maps** and **Route 66-specific apps** (such as **Route 66 Navigator** or **Roadside America**) are essential for real-time directions and up-to-date information.
    - **Tip:** Download offline maps or specific Route 66 apps in case you lose signal in more remote areas.
2. **Route 66 Signs and Landmarks**

- **What to Know:** Route 66 is marked by distinctive blue and white **Route 66 signs**, but the highway can split or follow parallel roads in certain areas. Look for signs along the way, but also pay attention to local landmarks, which are often key indicators of where you are on the route.
- **Tip:** Take note of mile markers or town names as you go. These will help you gauge your progress and keep you on track.

3. **Time Zones and Distance**
   - **What to Know:** As you travel through multiple states, you'll encounter different time zones. Be aware of time zone changes, especially when planning meals or stops along the way.
   - **Tip:** The trip from Chicago to Santa Monica takes roughly 10-12 days depending on how many stops you make, but don't rush it. Plan to spend a night or two in key towns along the way.

Gas Stations and Rest Stops

While Route 66 is full of iconic stops, you'll also want to be mindful of gas stations and rest areas along the way. Some parts of the highway pass through remote areas, and it's essential to stay fueled and refreshed.

1. **Fueling Up**
   - **What to Know:** Gas stations along Route 66 can be spaced out in more rural areas. Plan to stop and fill up whenever you're near a gas station to avoid running low on fuel in less populated sections.

- **Tip:** Always check your fuel gauge, and try to refuel when you're around a populated area, especially when driving through the desert or remote towns.

2. **Rest Stops**
   - **What to Know:** Rest stops are essential for stretching your legs and taking breaks from driving. Many of these stops are part of the highway's charm and include quirky roadside attractions, historical markers, or local parks.
   - **Tip:** Use rest stops as an opportunity to take photos, stretch, and enjoy the scenery. Many of these stops have clean restrooms, picnic areas, and sometimes even small shops or diners.

3. **Gas Station Services**
   - **What to Know:** Many gas stations along Route 66 offer more than just fuel. Look for places that provide snacks, drinks, and even local souvenirs. Some stations may also have ATM access, phone charging stations, or public Wi-Fi.
   - **Tip:** Take a moment to chat with the local attendants—they often have great insider knowledge on nearby attractions and the best spots to visit along the road.

Dealing with Weather and Emergencies

The weather along Route 66 can vary dramatically depending on the time of year and the regions you're passing through. It's essential to stay informed and be prepared for unexpected weather conditions, as well as emergencies.

1. **Weather Conditions**

- What to Expect: The climate along Route 66 can be extremely diverse. Expect hot and dry weather in Arizona and New Mexico, colder temperatures in the Midwest, and occasional rainstorms in the Midwest and West Coast.
- Tip: Pack clothing that can handle temperature changes, and always have extra water, especially in desert regions.

2. Emergency Kits
   - What to Pack: Always have an emergency kit in your vehicle, including a first aid kit, flashlight, phone charger, blankets, non-perishable food, and extra water. If you're driving in more remote sections, it's also a good idea to carry a spare tire, tire jack, and basic tools.
   - Tip: Cell phone service can be spotty in some areas, so carry a portable power bank and ensure your phone is fully charged before entering isolated stretches of road.

3. Dealing with Unexpected Weather
   - What to Know: Sudden storms can occur along Route 66, especially in the Midwest and Southwest. Be prepared for flash flooding in desert areas or snowstorms in higher elevations.
   - Tip: Always check the weather forecast before heading out, and adjust your plans accordingly if severe weather is expected.

4. Emergency Contacts and Services
   - What to Know: Make sure you have emergency contact numbers saved, including local roadside assistance, a family member or friend, and your vehicle insurance provider.

- **Tip:** In case of an emergency, most towns along Route 66 have a hospital or urgent care center, though rural areas may have limited services. It's always helpful to know where the nearest hospital is.

Money-Saving Tips

Traveling along Route 66 doesn't have to break the bank. Here are some practical tips to help you save money while still having an unforgettable trip.

1. **Plan Your Route**
   - **What to Do:** While Route 66 spans over 2,400 miles, you don't have to follow the highway's exact path at every turn. Research alternate routes or detours that may offer shorter travel times and lower fuel costs.
   - **Tip:** Use navigation apps like **Google Maps** to compare routes and check for traffic delays, road closures, or construction.
2. **Pack Your Own Snacks and Drinks**
   - **What to Do:** Stop at local grocery stores or convenience stores to stock up on snacks and beverages for the road. Buying snacks along the way at gas stations and diners can be expensive, and packing your own can help you save money.
   - **Tip:** Make sure to carry a cooler with bottled water, fresh fruit, sandwiches, and snacks to avoid constantly spending on fast food.
3. **Look for Budget Accommodations**
   - **What to Do:** You don't always have to stay in expensive hotels or resorts. Motels,

campgrounds, and even **hostels** (in larger cities) are great budget-friendly options.
- **Tip:** Use booking websites like **Hotels.com**, **Booking.com**, or **Airbnb** to find affordable stays along the route. Some motels may even offer discounts for extended stays or last-minute bookings.

4. **Take Advantage of Free Attractions**
   - **What to Do:** Many attractions along Route 66, such as **historic landmarks, state parks**, and **scenic viewpoints**, are free to visit. Plan your trip around free attractions that will give you the authentic Route 66 experience without spending a penny.
   - **Tip:** Many towns also host free festivals, parades, or outdoor concerts—check local event calendars for free entertainment along the way.

5. **Travel Off-Peak**
   - **What to Do:** Traveling during the shoulder seasons (spring and fall) rather than the summer can help you avoid higher prices for accommodations, attractions, and even dining.
   - **Tip:** Hotels and attractions tend to be cheaper during weekdays compared to weekends, so try to plan your route around these periods.

Conclusion

As we reach the end of this Route 66 Travel Guide 2025, I want to take a moment to thank you for allowing this guide to be a part of your journey along the Mother Road. Together, we've explored the diverse landscapes, rich history, and unique culture that make Route 66 so iconic. From the bustling streets of Chicago to the sun-drenched shores of Santa Monica, we've uncovered the treasures this historic highway has to offer.

Throughout these pages, we've ventured into the heart of America, witnessing the quirky charm of small towns, the striking beauty of national parks, and the vibrant spirit of Route 66's unforgettable landmarks. We've tasted classic diner meals, marveled at neon signs, and discovered hidden gems along the way. My hope is that this guide has not only helped you plan your road trip but also sparked a deeper appreciation for the soul of Route 66—the road that connects us to the past and fuels the adventurous spirit that lives within us all.

Route 66 is more than just a highway—it's a journey through time. It's the thrill of cruising along a historic road that's been traveled by millions, the joy of discovering a local diner with an endless history, and the magic of stopping at a roadside attraction that's as nostalgic as it is surprising. These are the moments that make this road trip so special—moments that remind us to embrace the freedom of the open road and the memories we create along the way.

As you travel Route 66, I encourage you to embrace its unpredictability. Take time to wander off the beaten path, chat with locals, and discover those hidden gems that don't always make the guidebooks. Some of the best experiences are the unexpected ones—the roadside stop you almost missed, the small-town festival you didn't plan for, or the quiet moment when the world feels just a little bit slower.

Thank you again for choosing this Route 66 Travel Guide 2025 to accompany you on your adventure. I hope it's given you the practical tips you need and, most importantly, the inspiration to hit the road with a sense of wonder and curiosity. Route 66 has a way of leaving an impression on all who travel it, and I trust it will stay with you long after your journey ends.

Safe travels, fellow road tripper. May your time on Route 66 be filled with adventure, discovery, and unforgettable moments. And who knows? Maybe our paths will cross one day on that iconic stretch of road, as we continue to chase the spirit of Route 66 together. Until then, enjoy the ride!

Made in the USA
Coppell, TX
21 May 2025

49663311R00066